CW00449462

25 YEARS of...............
RAILWAY............
RESEARCH........

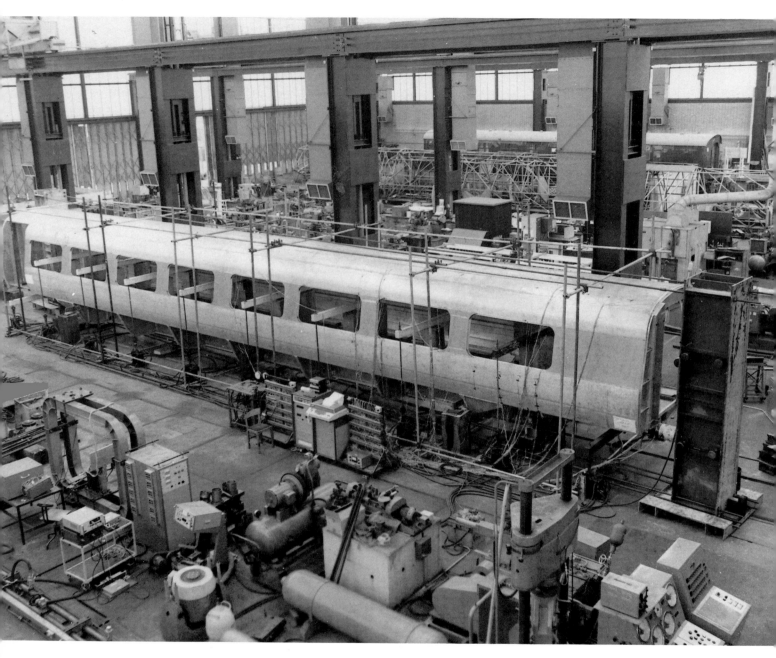

View of vehicle structure testing inside the Engineering Test Hall. The coach under test is a pre-production APT-P trailer vehicle, which was later used as the test car *Pilot*.

BR

25 YEARS OF............... RAILWAY............ RESEARCH.......

Colin J. Marsden

Haynes

Oxford Publishing Co.

Contents

The mainstay of Research motive power for many years was former Class 24 No. D5061 (24061), which in later years became Class 97/2 No. 97201, and sported the Research Division's red and blue livery. No. 97201 with the Research Tribology train is seen at Old Dalby in mid-1987.

A FOULIS-OPC Railway Book

© 1989 C.J. Marsden & Haynes Publishing Group

British Library Cataloguing in Publication Data
Marsden, C. J. (Colin J.)
25 years of railway research.
1. Great Britain. Railway services –
research organisations. Railway Technical
Centre
I. Title
385'.072041
ISBN 0-86093-441-1

Published by:
Haynes Publishing Group
Sparkford, near Yeovil, Somerset BA22 7JJ.

Haynes Publications Inc.
861 Lawrence Drive, Newbury Park, California 91320, USA.
Printed by J.H. Haynes & Co. Ltd.

Introduction

Twenty-five years ago in May 1964, British Rail Research – otherwise known as the Research Division – came into being at Derby with the opening of new purpose-built facilities at the Railway Technical Centre. Since then other facilities have been added to provide what is now recognised throughout the world as a centre of excellence for research into science and technology.

As well as providing BR with a cohesive research capability – with key objectives of helping to secure future traffic, reduce operating costs, and improve revenue – the Division undertakes consultancy work and studies for a wide range of external organisations, including other research establishments, overseas railways and the United Kingdom railway manufacturing industry.

There is an extensive and impressive range of test facilities available in the form of fixed hardware at Derby and the outbased Regional laboratories, as well as a number of mobile laboratory vehicles which can operate to virtually any part of the railway network.

This title, *25 years of Railway Research*, is the first book dedicated entirely to the Research Division. It does not set out to be an inventory of every research operation, but text and photographs have been selected to illustrate some of the different aspects of the complex nature of work carried out, together with details of test tracks and vehicles.

The production of this book has been helped by the assistance of the Director, Research, and his staff, and for this a special note of thanks must be recorded. It is hoped that the research facilities and operations detailed in this book will give readers an insight into the importance of British Rail Research. It should be noted that resources do not permit individual or party visits to any of the facilities described.

As an author and life-long railway enthusiast, with a special interest in technical and engineering matters, this book has been a most enjoyable undertaking and it is hoped that the readers will find it equally absorbing.

Colin J. Marsden
Dawlish

General view of the BR Research Division Headquarters Kelvin House, taken shortly after construction and forming part of the Railway Technical Centre in London Road, Derby.

BR

Note: As from 1st April 1989 BR Research has been reorganised as a self-accounting unit with its own annual business plan. Its relationships within British Rail are placed on a contractual basis and its ability to market its skills and technical expertise to the outside world has been strengthened.

The most prestigious, and highly publicised project undertaken by BR Research was the Advanced Passenger Train – the APT-E. The four-coach formation runs alongside the M1 motorway on the outskirts of London during a series of main line test runs in October 1974.

The Railway Technical Centre

Derby

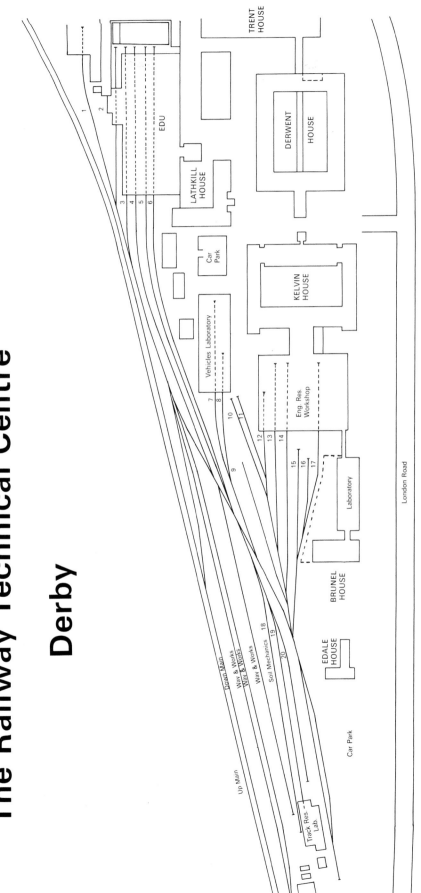

The Development of Derby Research

BR Research occupies part of the Railway Technical Centre (RTC), located in London Road, Derby. The RTC stands on the edge of the former township of Litchurch, the roots of which can be traced back to Saxon times. In the latter part of the 18th century the land was used for market gardens and woodland, with one of the owners being a William J. Etches, a famous Derby cheese factor, who occupied a small warehouse near the town's Midland Railway station.

Part of Etches' land was later turned into pleasure grounds which became known locally as Etches Park. In 1863 the prosperous Midland Railway Company purchased most of Etches' estate and erected a carriage shed and small coach workshop. Other parts of Etches' land were later used for the construction of 'Way and Works' department sidings, this section catering for buildings and non 'railway' items, and became the Central Stores for the entire area. The 'Way and Works' section gradually grew and by the early years of the 20th century had several buildings which were rail connected, administration offices and stabling sidings. Another part of the original Etches land was used to construct a new rail route, avoiding the need for trains from the north having to reverse before heading south.

Railway research in Derby can be traced back to 1841 when the Midland Counties engine *Bee* was fitted with 'Samuel Hills Patent Smoke Consuming Apparatus', which consisted of six steam lower boiler tubes being extended through the smokebox to a bell-mounted opening at the front of the engine, other additional fittings included eight cross tubes through the firebox walls and a steam blower in the chimney. Further research on this locomotive was carried out at a later date when a brick arch was added in an attempt to conform to the Government's instruction which prohibited smoke emission, but still required the company to use coal and not coke. Regrettably the Hall experiments were not totally successful, with further experimental work carried out by Matthew Kirtley in 1859, the then Midland Locomotive and Wagon Superintendent, a man who eventually solved the problem by combining the brick arch with a firehole door deflector plate and a blower.

The world famous railway engineer Robert Stephenson also carried out a small amount of research at Derby, mainly into smokebox temperatures in the early half of the 19th century.

In the early 1850s research into severe track wear was undertaken by Robert Forester Mushet who eventually produced the first double-headed steel rail using Bessemer steel. The product of this research work was later laid near Derby station in 1857, which unlike the former cast iron rails which lasted only six months, were still in use in 1873.

An experiment which had long lasting effects on rail traction was conducted by the Workshop Manager, Mr F. Holt, in 1886, when he researched and devised a system of applying sand or grit between wheel and rail, in an attempt to improve adhesion. This method of sanding, although using steam as its power source, has been refined in many ways and is still used today, the steam being replaced by compressed air.

In 1870-71, following a number of serious wrought iron axle failures, Mr Matthew Kirtley carried out major research into this subject which, after many years, led to the introduction of steel axles.

A separate Engineering Testing Department was formed under the control of Samuel Johnson towards the end of the 19th century, within the Locomotive Works, with facilities for structure testing up to 50 tons. Measuring equipment for this was invented and produced by Richard Mountford Deeley, a highly respected scientist, who in his later years succeeded Johnson as MR Locomotive Superintendent.

In 1910 further research facilities were formed near to Derby Locomotive Works at Calvert Street, when a Textile Research Station was opened for the observation, wear testing and quality assurance of MR upholstery and materials.

After the railway Grouping in 1923, and the absorption of various railway companies to form the London Midland & Scottish Railway (LMSR), it was decided to concentrate most of the company's research and exploratory operations at Derby, a move masterminded by the then Company President, Lord Stamp, who in 1929 presented a paper to the Institute of Transport entitled "Scientific Research in Transport". In 1930 Lord Stamp was the founder of the Advisory Committee on Scientific Research for Railways.

During the early 1930s the various LMS Paint and Varnish Laboratories were amalgamated, and in 1933 were absorbed into the LMS Scientific Research Laboratory formed by Sir Harold Hartley CBE, FRS, at the time Director of Scientific Research and a Vice-President of the LMS. To provide accommodation for the new Scientific section, purpose built Research Department buildings were designed by H.J. Connal, FRIBA, of the LMS Chief Engineers Department, comprised of a two-storey block of some 5,600sq ft floor space. Adjoining this basically laboratory area was a test hall and workshop of 3,500sq ft. The buildings were steel framed with reinforced floors and roof. Construction of the building was carried out by Greenwoods of Mansfield, with fittings supplied by F. Jackson & Co. Opening of the Centre was on 10th December 1935, with the ceremony conducted by Lord Rutherford of Nelson in company with Lord Stamp. The new Research building housed sections dealing with Metallurgy, Textiles, Paint and general Engineering Research, each section having a sizeable office and laboratory section. The total staff at the new centre located in London Road was just over 150, of which 60 were scientific graduates.

A wide brief was given to the new Research Unit, not only were responsibilities held for the study of metallurgy and chemical analysis, but virtually all technical areas of the railway were covered. This included a section which liaised with outside scientific and research bodies and many universities which had technical cores. A small group within the new Section dealt with advancing the railway with the emphasis being placed on the development of prototypes and the use of new materials, and most important of all, the testing of new designs, using mobile test units, test trains and dynamometer cars.

In 1935 the then head of the LMS Research & Engineering Section Dr F.C. Johansen, was told to form a

Early days of railway research: this superb view shows LMS "Baby Scot" No. 5533 standing outside the LMS paint shop at Crewe Works during the late 1930s, wired up to LMS dynamometer car No. 45052 prior to a series of controlled road tests. Note the additional front end cowling provided to house some of the testing staff.

BR

All regions of British Railways operated their own performance research undertakings until the formation of the BR Research operation in the mid-1960s. This view shows former GWR 'Hall' class 4-6-0 No. 7916 *Mobberley Hall* with front end cowling for engineers' observation. The train is seen at Wantage Road on 29th May 1951 during performance tests between Old Oak Common and Bristol. The vehicle behind the locomotive is the GWR dynamometer car.

Author's Collection

group to delve into aerodynamic forces, and for this a self-contained laboratory was formed in the Locomotive Works – prior to the final design stage of William Stanier's 'Coronation' 4-6-2 locomotives. After this work the Section dealt with further aerodynamic tests on the shaping of a streamlined articulated diesel unit. In both cases the research work involved the use of a 1/24 scale model. Such was the success of the Aero-dynamics Unit that the Lab was used for further trials in the years ahead. Significant testing included efficiency of smoke deflectors, design and positioning of coach roof ventilators, the size and positioning of diesel locomotive air louvres, and the wind pressures/resistances on stations and public by passing trains. By the early 1950s the Laboratory was moved to spare accommodation in the Carriage Works, where it continued although modified, until 1960, when it moved to the Derby College of Technology. It must not pass without record that the details above are in respect of Derby and the LMS alone. However, all railway companies had separate investigative and research functions, many of which continued in their own way long after Nationalisation in 1948.

A joint venture of the LMS and the LNER was the Rugby Locomotive Testing Station, which opened in Autumn 1948. This provided the first major locomotive testing and research facility and was, of course, used by all sections of the new BTC system. Right up until the mid 1960s, when the present BR Research Unit was formed, each of the regions, under the auspices of their relevant CM&EE operated experimental sections using various dynamometer and test trains, which provided invaluable assistance to the design departments.

In the post nationalisation years there was much discussion on the forming of a specialised BR Research Department. The first definite move in this direction came in September 1961 when a £1.25 million contract was placed for a major Engineering Laboratory to be built at Derby. The site chosen for this development being on the opposite side of London Road to the LMS research establishment, was on former LMS owned land, bounded by the Derby-Trent line, London Road and Dedmans Lane, and occupied largely by the Way and Works sidings. After the announcement in September 1961 it became clear that the new development was aimed at steering the railway design and research operation into the mechanised, electronic and computer age, which was just around the corner. The name given to the major Derby development was the Railway Technical Centre.

Before the days of the Railway Technical Centre, some of the research and performance tests were carried out at Rugby Testing Station or at the Mechanical & Electrical Engineering Test Division at Darlington. During 1957 the English Electric gas turbine prototype No. GT3 is seen undergoing high speed running on the famous Rugby Test Rollers.

GEC Traction

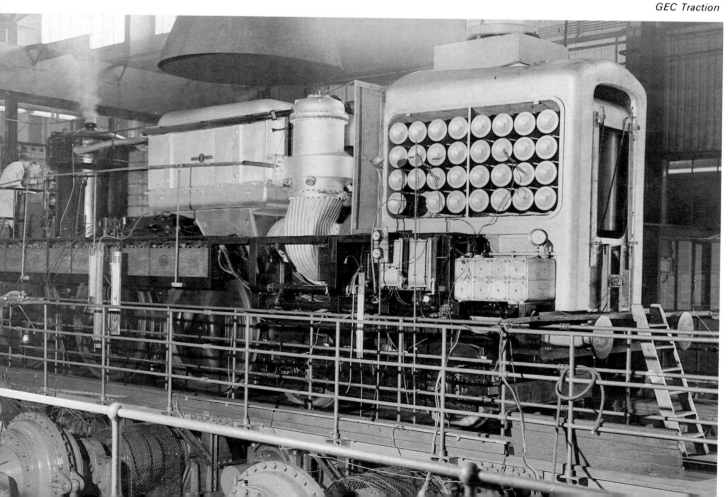

The building now known as Hartley House, on the opposite side of London Road to the Railway Technical Centre, is part of the original LMS Research and Scientific Laboratory, opened by the LMSR in December 1935. This illustration shows a general view of the building with the main entrance at the far end.

BR

The LMS Research building was officially opened on 10th December 1935 by Lord Rutherford of Nelson, OM, FRS. The opening party is seen after disembarking from their special train, and the principal gentlemen illustrated are, from left to right: Mr W. Allan Reid MP, Sir William Bragg, Lord Ashfield (rear), Sir Joshua Stamp, Sir Harold Hartley and Lord Rutherford.

BR

View of the LMS/BR Way and Works sidings adjacent to London Road in the early 1960s, prior to clearance of the land in readiness for the building of the Railway Technical Centre. The carriage sheds of Etches Park can be seen in the left background. This view of the Way and Works sidings was taken from the roof of the LMS Research building.

BR

Building the Site

Work began on developing the Derby site almost immediately after announcement of the project, with a contract for construction being drawn up in late September 1961.

The external design of the new complex was carried out by Dr F.F.C. Curtis, and Dr Ing FRIBA, of the BRB Architects Department. The plans called for the building of one main Engineering Test Hall, linked directly to a courtyard block – which on three sides comprised single storey laboratories and fronted onto the fourth by a five storey administration block. Construction of this, as well as the associated track installation, commenced during the third week of September, the main contractor being William Moss & Sons. At the time of contract, construction was set to take 26 months, however few problems were encountered within the build and construction was completed and the buildings handed over to BR in October 1963.

The main Engineering Test Hall included facilities for structural testing (for both vehicles and ancillary equipment), instrumentation of component parts as well as covered accommodation for the fitting out of test cars. A full description of this Test Hall is given in a later chapter. Although a number of the 100 research staff, which brought together personnel from the Electrical Research Division (formerly in London), the Mechanical Engineers Research Section, the Civil Engineering Research Unit, the Chemical Research Unit and the Scientific Services Division, started to occupy the site from the end of 1963, the BR Research Division was not formally opened until 14th May 1964 when HRH Prince Philip, The Duke of Edinburgh, performed the official opening. At the same time the main administration block was named Kelvin House after the famous scientist Sir William Kelvin.

Although not for BR Research, building work resumed at the Railway Technical Centre in 1965 when work commenced on a three storey block, later named Derwent House after the River Derwent. This was opened in March 1967 by the then Minister of Transport The Rt Hon. Mrs Barbara Castle MP. This building was to house the headquarters staff of the Workshops Division – later, from January 1970 British Rail Engineering Limited (BREL), as well as the Railway Board's Central Purchasing Department. Concurrent with the construction of Derwent House came the building of Trent House, a three storey quadrangled block for the occupancy of the various M&EE and Drawing Office Sections. A further M&EE building – the Engineering Development Unit (EDU) was added in 1966, to replace a previous facility at Darlington.

The next BR Research building to be commissioned was the Plastics Development Unit (PDU), designed by the BRB architects and built by Taylor Woodrow in 1966, comprising a central workshop, two storey laboratory area and office accommodation on three sides. The manning of the PDU was principally by the staff of the former Eastleigh based Plastics Section, together with some newly appointed staff members. This section was formed primarily to study and design possible applications for plastic, glass fibre and glass reinforced plastic in the railway industry. Perhaps their best known achievement was the designing

and building of the original High Speed Train (HST) air smoothed front ends. Other functions of the Department included work on overhead line masts, portable buildings and station materials.

In 1968 the then named Track Research and Soil Mechanics Group was formed, and provided with a test hall, office and laboratory accommodation. The design for this building was carried out by the BRB architects, construction being effected by Ford & Weston of Derby, with completion in 1969. This new facility comprised a test hall, with its own section of track, a two storey office block and laboratory. The building was, of course, rail connected enabling track machines or vehicles to be accommodated if required.

Further expansion of the Research Division came in 1966 when Lathkill House was built, named after the Derbyshire river and dale. The design was again by the BRB architects and construction performed by Taylor Woodrow. This building consisted of a three storey office unit and was built to house the Dynamics Group, Braking Systems Unit and the Vehicle Suspension Section.

The second largest of the Research Vehicle Laboratories was designed in 1968 by Mr A.B. Kaukas, Chief Architect, BRB, for the preparation and translation of Advanced Passenger Train theory into operational hardware. The building provided 16,200sq ft of floor area incorporating rail 'roads', workshop area and special elevated control room. The building, primarily a rectangle, was built by Taylor Woodrow Construction Ltd at a cost of £250,000. The completion of the building was in the autumn of 1970 and officially opened at the end of October by John Peyton, then Minister for Transport Industries. This laboratory was named The Advanced Projects Laboratory and placed under the control of the Director Advanced Projects. The contents of the laboratory, which included brake dynamometers, is fully described in a subsequent section.

A further sizeable office and laboratory was built in 1970 for the Field Trials, Fracture Mechanics, Aerodynamics, Instrumentation and Chemical Research units, as well as a Research Department Drawing Office. This block was named Brunel House, being designed by Mr A.B. Kaukas, built by Holland, Hannen & Cubitts and completed in the late summer of 1971. It was officially opened on 27th August by Sir Henry Johnson CBE, then Chairman of the British Railways Board.

Following the 1971 building no further purpose-built laboratory accommodation has been constructed for the Research Division at Derby. However in 1971, construction of a Research Division Library commenced in the courtyard of Kelvin House, which now provides a valuable source of technical reference material to all engineering disciplines, and is additionally used by all technical departments throughout the Railway Technical Centre. The Research Library was opened on 22nd June 1972 by Dr Sidney Jones, the original Director of Research, who was by then a non-executive member of the Railways Board.

Away from the main Railway Technical Centre, on the other side of London Road, the former LMS research buildings are now operated under the 'BR Research' banner, forming Hartley House and Faraday House, and are occupied by the Scientific Services Group, housing office and laboratory accommodation.

In addition to the main facilities two Research owned Test Tracks exist, one at Mickleover and the other at Old Dalby. Details of these are given in separate chapters later in this book.

At the end of September 1961 the contractor, William Moss, commenced clearing the former Way and Works yard prior to the construction of the new buildings. This illustration shows the view across London Road, again taken from the LMS building, looking towards the land on which now stands the Engineering Test Hall.

BR

Construction of the original Research building, now Kelvin House, and the Engineering Test Hall, continued throughout 1962 and 1963 with completion and handing over of the basic structure coming in October 1963. Kelvin House is seen from London Road in early 1964, prior to the construction of Derwent House, which was built on the temporary Kelvin House car park.

BR

These Laboratories were opened by
HIS ROYAL HIGHNESS
THE PRINCE PHILIP · DUKE OF EDINBURGH
on the fourteenth of May
nineteen sixty four

The official ceremony to open the Research Laboratories was held on 14th May 1964, when HRH The Prince Philip, Duke of Edinburgh, made an official visit to the Railway installations of Derby, visiting the Locomotive Works and opening Kelvin House and the Engineering Test Hall. These two illustrations show the Duke of Edinburgh unveiling the stone plaque in the entrance foyer of Kelvin House and signing the visitors' book, under the watchful eye of Dr Beeching.

Both: BR

The use of plastics and glass reinforced plastic has increased over recent years and during the late 1960s a Plastic Development Unit (PDU) was established. Much of the information obtained assisted in the production of the cabs for the prototype and production IC125s. In this picture a previously formed skirt is seen being fitted to an already manufactured front end.

BR

View of the outside of Lathkill House built by Taylor Woodrow in 1966 to house the Dynamics, Braking and Vehicle Suspension groups.

Built in 1969-70, the Advanced Projects Laboratory was constructed by Taylor Woodrow, to house the Advanced Passenger Train project. In later years the building has been used to provide covered accommodation for the expanding field of general railway research.

The 1970 completion of the Advanced Projects Laboratory (now Vehicles Laboratory) heralded the start of the major APT development operation. The opening of the Advanced Projects Laboratory was conducted by the Rt. Hon. John Peyton MP – Minister for Transport Industries – seen unveiling the plaque fixed to the wall of the Laboratory control room.

Author's Collection

ADVANCED PROJECTS LABORATORY

This building was opened by The Rt. Hon. John Peyton, M.P. Minister for Transport Industries

26 TH OCTOBER 1970

In 1971 a Research Division Library was built in the courtyard to the rear of Kelvin House, housing an invaluable reference source for staff of all RTC functions. The building is viewed from the Kelvin courtyard with the main doors towards the right.

BR

When originally opened the rear of Kelvin House contained four stabling sidings, where some of the Division's vehicles were kept, in latter years this area formed part of the Advanced Projects Laboratory. The garage block, seen in the background, was later re-positioned to make way for other buildings.

BR

General view of the LMS built research building, now forming Hartley and Faraday Houses of the present research complex. Note the LMS insignia above the near door.

General layout of original Research site.

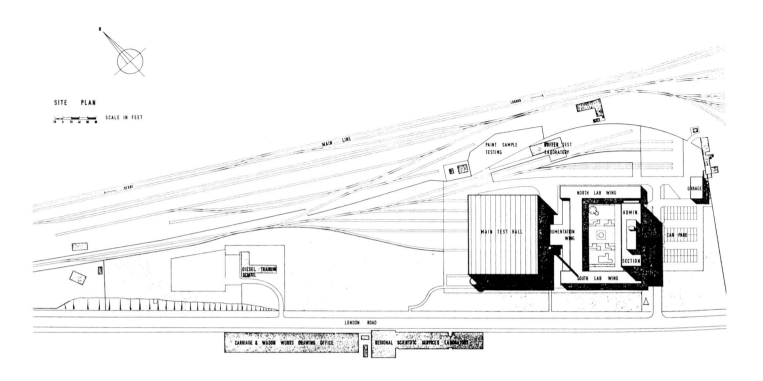

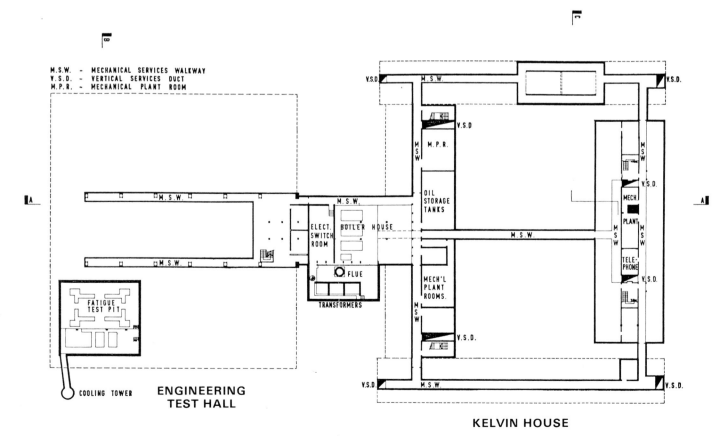

M.S.W. — MECHANICAL SERVICES WALKWAY
V.S.D. — VERTICAL SERVICES DUCT
M.P.R. — MECHANICAL PLANT ROOM

ENGINEERING
TEST HALL

KELVIN HOUSE

**Basement plan of Engineering Test Hall
and Kelvin House – 1964.**

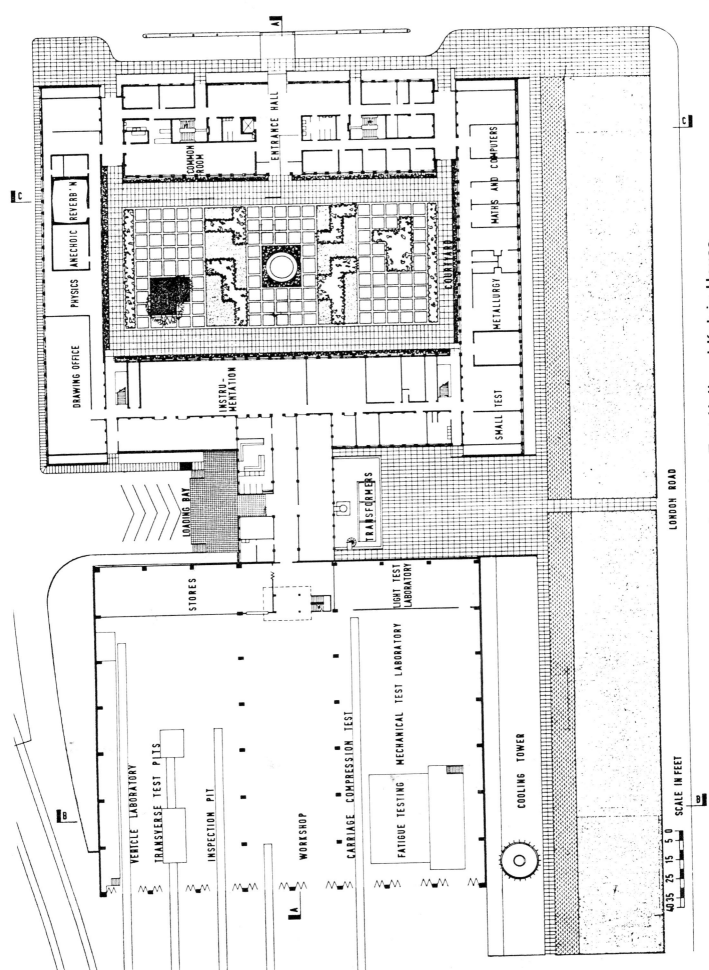

Ground floor plan of Engineering Test Hall and Kelvin House

VEHICLE LABORATORY

TRANSVERSE TEST PITS

INSPECTION PIT

WORKSHOP

CARRIAGE COMPRESSION TEST

FATIGUE TESTING MECHANICAL TEST LABORATORY

COOLING TOWER

STORES

LOADING BAY

LIGHT TEST LABORATORY

TRANSFORMERS

DRAWING OFFICE

PHYSICS

ANECHOIC

REVERB'N

COMMON ROOM

ENTRANCE HALL

INSTRU-MENTATION

COURTYARD

MATHS AND COMPUTERS

METALLURGY

SMALL TEST

LONDON ROAD

SCALE IN FEET

40 35 25 15 5 0

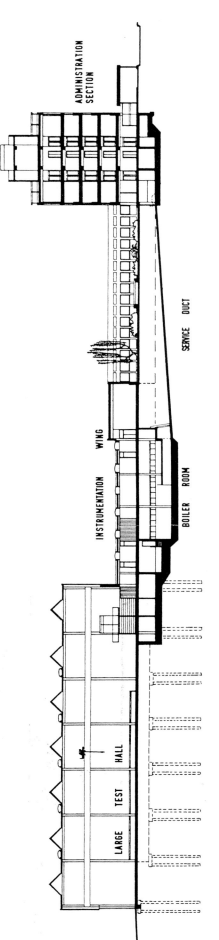

Section A-A of Engineering Test Hall, Quadrangle and Kelvin House.

ADMINISTRATION SECTION

INSTRUMENTATION WING

SERVICE DUCT

BOILER ROOM

LARGE TEST HALL

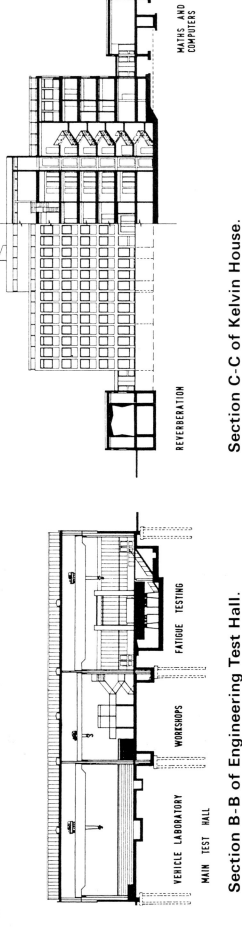

MATHS AND COMPUTERS

Section C-C of Kelvin House.

REVERBERATION

SCALE IN FEET

40 35 25 15 5 0

Section B-B of Engineering Test Hall.

FATIGUE TESTING

WORKSHOPS

VEHICLE LABORATORY

MAIN TEST HALL

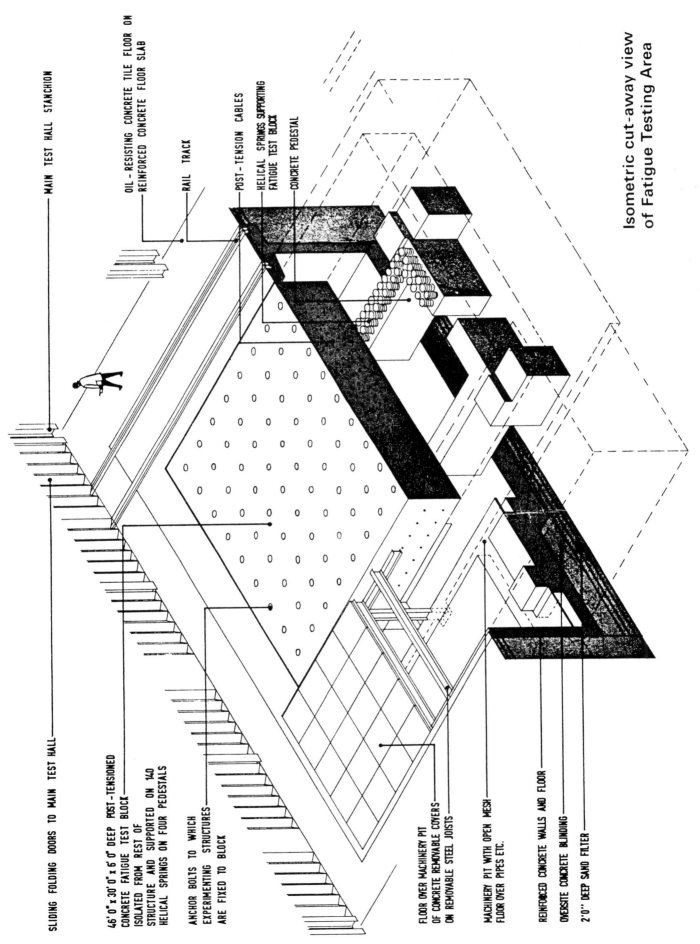

MAIN TEST HALL STANCHION

OIL - RESISTING CONCRETE TILE FLOOR ON REINFORCED CONCRETE FLOOR SLAB

RAIL TRACK

POST-TENSION CABLES

HELICAL SPRINGS SUPPORTING FATIGUE TEST BLOCK

CONCRETE PEDESTAL

Isometric cut-away view of Fatigue Testing Area

SLIDING FOLDING DOORS TO MAIN TEST HALL

46' 0" x 30' 0" x 6' 0" DEEP POST-TENSIONED CONCRETE FATIGUE TEST BLOCK ISOLATED FROM REST OF STRUCTURE AND SUPPORTED ON 140 HELICAL SPRINGS ON FOUR PEDESTALS

ANCHOR BOLTS TO WHICH EXPERIMENTING STRUCTURES ARE FIXED TO BLOCK

FLOOR OVER MACHINERY PIT OF CONCRETE REMOVABLE COVERS ON REMOVABLE STEEL JOISTS

MACHINERY PIT WITH OPEN MESH FLOOR OVER PIPES ETC.

REINFORCED CONCRETE WALLS AND FLOOR

OVERSITE CONCRETE BLINDING

2'0" DEEP SAND FILTER

21

One of the early areas of rail transport given attention by the Research Division was the system of linear induction motors, developed by Professor Laithwaite of Imperial College, London. An early system of linear propelled 'train' is seen in the Research yard on the day of its official opening, being explained to HRH Prince Philip.

BR

This view of the Engineering Test Hall shows the then Superintendent Dynamics Section Mr Alan Wickens (left), showing HRH Prince Philip and the official party a 12 ton box van attached to a hydraulic ram, which is applying side pressure to test suspension equipment.

BR

Some Principal Past Projects

Since the conception of the BR Research Division there have been many thousands of individual projects undertaken. Some have been purely paper undertakings, but the majority have graduated to the production of operational hardware. This section can in no way document all the past projects, as a tabular list alone would extend to several hundred pages, thus the following pages cover eight of the more important projects.

1. Magnetic Suspension Studies (MAG-LEV)

BR Research Division's assessment of magnetic suspension technology started in early 1973 as a direct result of a study contract from the British Government. Backed by the extensive facilities and experience of one of the world's leading railway technical laboratories, studies were made of both high and low speed transport applications, in terms of advantages and technical problems. Research showed that for high speed use, magnetic suspension did not appear to offer sufficient advantages to make it an automatic choice when compared with conventional wheel/rail systems.

At lower speeds however, many advantages could be identified and BR Research decided to construct a full scale prototype vehicle and special test 'track' at their Derby base in order to develop the necessary control systems, establish reliability levels of the concept and to demonstrate the ability of the system, including the smooth, silent movement of the vehicle even on sharply curved and graded routes.

The Derby Research MAG-LEV experimental vehicle, built in 1974, demonstrated the application of magnetic suspension, which removed the need for wheels, springs and dampers. The prototype vehicle was 3.5m long and weighed some 3 tonnes. A total of eight electro-magnets guided and powered the vehicle and held it in a levitated state. A linear induction system was provided for power and

braking, electric current for levitation and propulsion being collected via side collector arms. When MAG-LEV was levitated a gap of 15mm was maintained irrespective of the weight within the vehicle, between the base of the vehicle and the trackbed.

To evaluate MAG-LEV, and to confirm theories that the vehicle had the ability to negotiate tortuous routes, a 100m long test track was built in the Research yard. This incorporated 8m radius curves, and a gradient of 1:20. The trackbed was formed of reinforced concrete supporting steel rails, the rails being 50mm wide and of laminated construction. The total track gauge was 1.2m.

The Derby test programme demonstrated that magnetic suspension systems can provide a virtually silent, reliable transport system with very low maintenance and running costs, offering an ability to negotiate sharp curves and steep gradients with the added advantage of not being affected by bad weather conditions.

The fundamental research work carried out by the BR Research team, and the ensuing technical confidence and experience in MAG-LEV operations, was later applied to a fully operational system at Birmingham International Airport when BR Research acted as technical consultants to the group.

2. Low Cost Radio Signalling (R.E.T.B.)

In response to the need for a modern low-cost, but still highly reliable signalling system, with the same order of integrity as that provided by existing systems, BR Research,

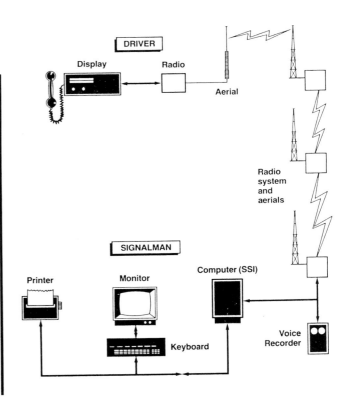

in conjunction with the signalling and operations departments developed a 'Radio Electronic Token Block' (RETB) system. The system is most suitable for signalling more lightly used single or double track sections, where the cost of employing several staff at often inaccessible outstations is outweighed by the provision of the RETB system. This comparatively modern signalling development uses radio communications and computer based signal interlockings, both in themselves BR Research studies.

The RETB system concentrates all the interlocking hardware and control equipments in one signal box and has achieved dramatic savings in costs of procurement, train running and maintenance costs.

To operate the RETB system it is necessary to fit the locomotive or multiple unit with either permanent or portable radio signal and display equipment. The controlling signal box is fitted with equipment to permit conventional signalling to interface with the RETB control equipment.

The first application of RETB was in Scotland, from Dingwall to Kyle of Lochalsh, Wick and Thurso. This was followed by installations in East Anglia, on the West Highland lines and in Wales.

3. Railbus

To answer the world-wide need for a low-cost rail passenger vehicle, BREL, the passenger vehicle division of Leylands and BR Research, jointly set about the development of the Railbus project. This called for the marrying of a rail underframe and a bus style body structure. At an early stage it was envisaged that up to 100 passengers could be transported in railbus vehicles at speeds of up to 75mph. After the project was authorised BR Research bought a body formed of two cabs fitted back to back with a few modules of body section formed between them, and thus the 'Railbus' was born. After building by the Research Division the vehicle became known as LEV 1 and was loaned to the US Federal Railroad Administration to perform tests on the Boston & Maine Railroad. For its operation in the US mesh windscreen guards were fitted. After return from the US 'Railbus' was numbered RDB975874 and operated on a number of secondary and branch lines during the course of development of 'new generation' rural rail vehicles.

After extensive trials had been completed, production orders for 4-wheel chassis Railbus type vehicles were placed, eventually leading to nearly 150 2-car sets being in operation. Railbus started life as a joint Research/private sector operation, which later became a BRE/private sector production undertaking.

4. Structure Gauging Train

BR Research completed a Rapid Structure Gauging train for the Director of Civil Engineering in the summer of 1986, a project which had been in the development stage for many months.

Adequate clearances must exist between rolling stock and lineside structures to ensure total safety. To guarantee that these minimal tolerances are maintained structure gauging takes place. Previously structure gauging had been a time-consuming and tedious job, using wooden gauging frames or a vehicle mounted feeler system. However, with the present advances in electronic and measuring equipment, BR operators required a structure gauge measuring train which could gauge the network at speeds up to 30mph, and accurately record the route co-ordinates or lineside structures up to 10ft either side of the track centre line.

Research took the project on board in the early 1980s and developed a purpose-built vehicle with a mounted automatic television measuring system, which exceeded the basic requirements in terms of its maximum recording speed and scope of coverage. On close structures the accuracy on the horizontal plane is within $\pm$ $1/2$ in. The measurement system incorporated was a dual triangulation arrangement in which pairs of television cameras, mounted either side of an isoplanar illumination system, measure the angle at which light enters the cameras after being scattered by a lineside structure. The illumination system uses conventional tungsten-halogen lamps and this restricts operation of the vehicle to the hours of darkness. Fortunately this is not a serious operational problem as most of the suitable pathways are in the night hours.

The vehicle mounted system measures the profiles of the lineside structures using the vehicle as a measuring base. Simultaneous measurements are made of the vehicle attitude with respect to the track, so that the measurement may be converted to a required frame of reference which is used on the track position.

To aid the off-line analysis of the gauging data, an infra-red television system records the view from the driver's cab, this allows superfluous infringements of the structure gauge, ie over-growing trees etc, to be identified and edited out of the records prior to their transfer to the Central Data Base.

In addition to gauging, the vehicle measures track cant, curvature and 6 foot clearances, as well as movement position calculated every 15 feet, all this additional data being recorded digitally on magnetic tape.

The structure gauging vehicle, No. 460000 is formed as the middle car of a 3-vehicle formation, the two outer coaches housing computer data collection and riding facilities. The set whilst under development was operated by the Director of Research, but was later handed over to the Director of Civil Engineering.

5. The V-Laser

Research developed a new concept in laser control of construction plant known as the V-Laser. This is a totally machine-mounted system which can radically improve the performance of levelling or smoothing plant over the surface wavelength ranges. The machine also extends the effectiveness to wavelengths otherwise restricted by basic geometrical limitations such as wheelbase.

Unlike the more usual laser based systems, which provide an absolute straight line or flat plane datum, the V-Laser results in a surface in which small scale undulations are eliminated but which conforms to the existing large scale topography. The system basically consists of shining a low output laser onto the ground ahead of the mobile tracked vehicle and using the image of the spot to monitor the height of the surface at this point, as the machine moves forward. This information is used to control the height of the blade in the same way that the front wheels of a grader control the height of its blade.

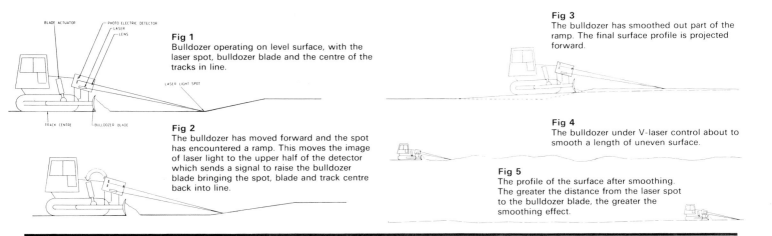

Fig 1
Bulldozer operating on level surface, with the laser spot, bulldozer blade and the centre of the tracks in line.

Fig 2
The bulldozer has moved forward and the spot has encountered a ramp. This moves the image of laser light to the upper half of the detector which sends a signal to raise the bulldozer blade bringing the spot, blade and track centre back into line.

Fig 3
The bulldozer has smoothed out part of the ramp. The final surface profile is projected forward.

Fig 4
The bulldozer under V-laser control about to smooth a length of uneven surface.

Fig 5
The profile of the surface after smoothing. The greater the distance from the laser spot to the bulldozer blade, the greater the smoothing effect.

6. PACT system of Concrete Slab Track

A major Research project was launched in the late 1960s into the development of a paved trackbed system, utilizing much previous knowledge of the road industry. The project was given the title PACT, with development being jointly undertaken by BR Research and McGregor (Paving) Ltd of Chesterfield. Both BR and industry were aware that the slip form technique of laying concrete jointless beds for road and airport runway applications was rapidly advancing, this coinciding with the Office de Recherches et d'Essais [ORE] of the International Union of Railways, addressing the question of 'Tracks Without Ballast' and seeking a suitable test site.

BR were therefore invited to construct the ORE test installation of paved track, which was carried out with close liaison between BR Research and McGregor Ltd. The site chosen for the ORE test was at Radcliffe-on-Trent on the Grantham – Nottingham line, where a total of four ORE, and three BR sections of paved track were installed, each being approximately 220ft in length and abutted to one another. Each of the sections were of slightly different characteristic, but all were assembled using a McGregor modified wire-guided slip form paver. Site construction commenced in July 1968 and was opened to traffic in April 1969.

Following the operation of the Radcliffe test section, it was decided that further research was justified in the BR based system, and with Channel Tunnel possibilities in mind, a second paved track installation was authorised, where high speed running with heavy axle loading could be monitored, the section of line used for this research programme was at Duffield, where a 1¼ mile section was built using a wire-guided paver vehicle.

Considerable research was subsequently undertaken into paved track research which culminated in paved trackbeds being installed in a number of locations, including Scotland, Wales, Ireland, Spain, New Zealand, Australia and South Africa.

7. Transponders

During the 1970s it became apparent that much additional information could be passed to trains and their drivers whilst in motion using a track-mounted 'beacon' or Transponder system. These between rail-mounted Transponders did not require any external power source and could relay information fed to them at the time of manufacture. This data would ideally be permanent speed restrictions or other important track layout information. To gauge the operation of this track equipment the Research Division converted a special test car *Mercury* to operate over the LM main line where track equipment had been installed. After many months of research in 1974 the Transponder system was developed into a data and speed restriction information system known as C-APT which was installed in the Euston-Glasgow route for APT Class 370 sets. Today this basic ground research is still being used in the development of track/train data links.

8. Sodium Sulphur Battery

BR Research started a major programme in 1967 into sodium sulphur cell technology, as part of a nationally co-ordinated programme of research sponsored by Government. Under this scheme, research was carried out by BR, Chloride Silent Power Ltd, and Harwell. In 1978 a major step forward in the production of a reliable rechargeable battery less than 1/5th the weight of the corresponding lead-acid type came when BR Research completed development of a 10kW/h sodium sulphur battery. The new battery was able to develop 45v from 176 cells, with a 288 A/h capacity.

By 1981 the development of the sodium sulphur battery had reached another major stage, when BR Research powered a road vehicle, using an 11kW/h battery.

Additional research into this subject is still continuing, with possibilities for traction usage continually being explored.

Space restrictions in this book have precluded detailed coverage of many other adventurous projects, including the development of: **High Speed Track Recording Car [HSTRC]**, built on a production Mk 2f vehicle, **Welding Research**, culminating in the development of safer continuous welded rail sections, **Overhead Power Equipment Research** leading to the present design of neutral sections, culminating in the overall reduction of bridge heights over energised sections. **Flashing Tail Light** equipment has now become available following years of research, with tail lamp units now operating with batteries that will last up to one year before replacement. **SR AWS** development of this advanced automatic warning system utilized an inductive loop system which gave actual signal displays of approached signals in the driver's cab.

The above are but a few of the interesting projects undertaken by BR Research since its formation 25 years ago. Most of these have had 'spin-off' projects and all have led to a safer and improved rail system.

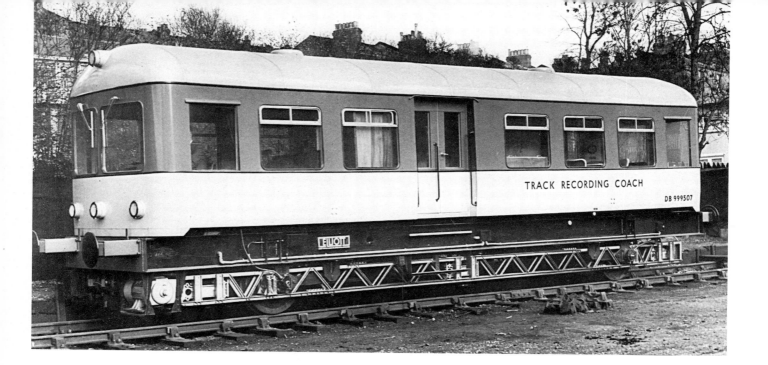

One of the first purpose-built test cars was the Wickham built *Elliott* track recording coach No. DB999507 which in fact emerged in 1958 prior to the formation of the Research Division, when the vehicle was operated by the Civil Engineers. *Elliott* was, in 1970, taken over by the Research team, where it is still used today as Lab No. 20. The upper view shows *Elliott* in 'as built' condition at Derby, while the lower illustration shows the vehicle passing Rowsley sidings in the Peak District, on a track assessment special on 2nd May 1963.

Author's Collection/R.W. Hawkins

An experiment during the summer of 1971 by the Research Division's Train Control Group, was carried out to demonstrate the technical feasibility of a system which was considered as a viable method of transporting single freight container wagons. The scheme, known as 'Autowagon', used a self-powered container wagon, which was projected to operate on its own, over the spare capacity of the rail network. For demonstration purposes 'Autowagon' was operated on the Division's research line at Mickleover where the vehicle, complete with a Freightliner container, is seen approaching the transfer frame.

BR

The experimental BR Research constructed 'MAG-LEV' vehicle, climbs the elevated section of the test track in the RTC complex yard. The elevating electro-magnets can be seen clearly.

The original Leyland Railbus body shell is shown in the Engineering Test Hall while structure testing was being carried out.
BR

The body shell, which eventually became LEV 1 is illustrated inside the Engineering Test Hall, separated from its 4-wheel chassis. On the left, car No. PC4 of the APT-POP train can be seen.

Ray Ruffell

Close up of wheel and suspension assembly of Leyland Experimental Vehicle (LEV 1).

BR

The High Speed Track Recording Coach (HSTRC) operated by the Director of Civil Engineering was built by BR Research on a body shell supplied by BREL Derby Litchurch Lane. HSTRC No. DB999550 is illustrated at Dawlish Warren in 1981, coupled to the rear of a service train. The vehicle has the ability to be operated within most train consists, including inter-coupling with IC125 stock.

General view of the purpose-built Structure Gauging Vehicle No. 460000, while under fitting out.

The APT-E Project

The Advanced Passenger Train – Experimental (APT-E) project had its roots back in the early 1960s, prior to the formation of the Railway Technical Centre (RTC), when a major project was authorised to discover how railway wheelsets of differing types performed on rails. This research programme was directed by Mr Alan Wickens, a graduate of Loughborough University, who joined British Rail in 1962, being previously employed in the aero-space industry. By 1964, when the RTC opened, a team had been formed to investigate wheel/rail dynamics, and in the ensuing years both mathematical models and computer predictions indicated that below a determinable critical speed, and following disturbance from the track, wheelsets underwent a decaying oscillation. Also, above a critical speed a vehicle becomes unstable with oscillation increasing, which eventually leads to hunting. The 'critical' speed of the wheelset was dependent on suspension parameters and on the design of future vehicles, especially if high speeds were desirable. This 'critical' speed had to be higher than the maximum operating speed.

A prototype High Speed Freight Vehicle (HSFV 1) No. RDB511023 was built after much laboratory testing, this being a Conflat with a significantly modified suspension system and wheelsets. HSFV 1 was operated under test conditions on the main lines and showed to be stable at speeds of up to 100mph. The vehicle was also subjected to roller speed tests where the wheels were rotated at up to 140mph. Results from both tests indicated that the Group's previous predictions were correct and thus it was now possible to design and build vehicles able to travel at speeds well over previous limits.

Concurrently with the suspension research other aspects of vehicle dynamics were under investigation, including the behaviour of vehicles on curves, and how wheels and bogies responded to track irregularities. Wheelsets, when traversing any curve, require the 'outer' wheel to travel faster than the 'inner'. This cannot happen of course with rigid wheelsets and thus slippage has to occur. Wheelsets with conical tyres overcame the slipping phenomenon by setting themselves radial to the curve, moving marginally outward so that conicity provides the rolling radius difference required. Wheelsets forming part of a vehicle will not usually have this freedom of movement, constraints being imposed by suspension. Forces applied to the wheelset through suspension are resisted by wheel/rail forces to a point of friction when slipping commences, with guidance of the wheelset then being provided by the wheel flanges.

To provide good curving characteristics it was necessary to impose low suspension stiffness and high conicity, this being the total opposite for a good stability, which called for stiff suspension – therefore a compromise was necessary for conventional configurations in which a certain critical speed is obtained at the expense of curving ability. The above experiments, all being installed and tested in HSFV 1, were carried out between 1965 and 1967. By 1967 a 'trial' application of the above theories was made on both main line and suburban stock.

Simultaneously with the above areas of research BR were very keen to improve the speed of their InterCity services. Proof had been provided in April 1966 with the Euston-Manchester/Liverpool electrification, that the improved schedules considerably increased line revenue and assisted BR in being competitive with the road and air market in linking the major cities. Market research showed that three major trunk routes, London-Edinburgh, London-Glasgow and London-Bristol/South Wales, were losing revenue to other transport forms, and that improved schedules would draw passengers back to the rail market.

Of course, other major rail administrations throughout the world were also introducing modern high speed city-city services, but for the majority 'new' purpose-built railway systems were constructed. However for the proposed British high speed era restraints prevented new railways being built and therefore designers were given the task of producing detailed plans of new trains and rolling stock able to travel at far faster speeds on existing railway track.

Research at Derby into the vehicle dynamics field provided data to produce a 'faster' locomotive and stock that could travel on straight tracks at significantly higher speed. However, as some 50% of the major routes were made up of curves where speed restrictions were imposed, more powerful locomotives would not answer all the problems. To provide the answer in increasing speeds throughout the network, a vehicle that could negotiate curves at nearer line speed was needed. The solution lay in a tilting vehicle which could lean to curves, thus reducing track and ride problems. Planners decreed that the West Coast Main Line (WCML) would benefit most from a tilting train, which would be able to negotiate the 401 1/4 miles between Euston and Glasgow in around 4 hours, although not exceeding 125mph. In comparison the East Coast Main Line (ECML) and the Paddington-South Wales route, would not significantly benefit from tilting trains, and a higher output conventional train would be more desirable.

By mid-1968 the BRB was faced with the problem of how to develop the next generation of express InterCity train, either to opt for the development of a tilting train or to use established rail principles for stock but increase the power output.

In 1969 the BRB authorised the construction of an experimental train to research and develop the concept of a tilting train, to become known as the Advanced Passenger Train – Experimental (APT-E). As the project was delving into new fields of engineering, where little research had been previously undertaken, and no fixed timescale could be given, the BRB also decided in 1970 to construct a prototype conventional train able to travel at speeds of up to 125mph on existing track; this project eventually became known as the High Speed Train (HST).

Between the time that the tilt system had been identified in 1968 as the best method of improving overall speeds, and the authorisation of APT-E construction, BR Research had achieved a considerable amount of work and collected valuable data on track, aerodynamics and acoustics. Many tests were carried out using HSFV 1, but eventually an APT-POP train was developed.

The 1969 BRB approval for the APT project called for the following major objectives:-

A. A 50% higher maximum speed.
B. A 40% higher curving speed.
C. To operate on existing tracks and within existing signal parameters.
D. A high standard of passenger comfort.
E. Energy efficiency.
F. Low noise levels.
G. To maintain existing schedules for track repair.
H. To maintain the 1969 figure of cost per seat-mile.

At the planning stage of APT-E it was identified that the propulsion system to be employed must have a high power to weight ratio. The potential was seen to use the gas-turbine system which offered greater flexibility in the projected testing programme than electric. Initially it was planned to utilise Rolls-Royce Dart engines but eventually the turbine type decided upon was the Leyland Automotive turbine, similar to that used in road vehicles. To achieve the required 2,400hp in the experimental train four 300hp turbines were to be positioned in each power car, with a fifth turbine providing power for auxiliaries.

Before construction was authorised for the 4-coach APT-E a number of fitments had to be decided upon, and this included the cant (tilt), brake and traction equipments.

Research previously undertaken showed that when a passenger train negotiates a curve the passengers are subjected to centrifugal force. To restrict this effect on passenger comfort, tracks are canted in curved areas by raising the outer rail, and although this assists with the problem, it only negates the centrifugal forces at one speed. In excess of the 'cant speed' passengers will be subjected to a level of centrifugal force, and at speeds below cant speed passengers would feel the pull of gravity. Many existing tracks in 1969 were canted for speeds less than the line speed limit, the force between cant speed and line speed being expressed as a 'cant deficiency' figure, ie if a train traverses a curve at 100mph, but it is only canted for 80mph, the cant deficiency would be 20mph. Under BR Safety Regulations the cant deficiency was limited to 4 degrees, this figure being widely accepted as the maximum public acceptance without discomfort, although research had shown that canting up to 9 degrees was practical with minor passenger discomfort. This led to the concept of a canting vehicle (tilting train), whereby if the vehicle body canted inwards at 9 degrees this would fully compensate for cant deficiency – thus giving a fully compensated ride on all existing curves and giving no passenger discomfort at far higher speeds than had previously been possible.

BR Research also carried out exhaustive tests into track damage caused by trains travelling at high speeds, the vertical track loading caused by static axle loads were insignificant, but the dynamic forces caused by trains at high speed were very important. To maintain the dynamic forces within tolerable levels the unsprung mass of the APT-E travelling at speeds of around 150mph had to be in the region of 1.5 tonnes. To meet this target a new transmission system would have been needed, but as the production lead-in time was very short, conventional axle-hung dc traction motors were used.

Another field of major research that had to be carried out prior to construction/testing of the experimental set, was a method of braking. The ability to reduce the speed and stop a train from 150mph was obviously available, but this stopping had to be within existing signalling distances. To achieve this target and meet the limits of unsprung mass, a new brake to the railway field had to be developed – the hydro-kinetic brake. The hydro-kinetic brake mounted within the hollow axles comprised two bladed members, one of which was held stationary whilst the other rotated with the wheels. When the brake was applied a special water glycol mixture was forced by air pressure from a reservoir into the blading, and the ensuing energy of motion of the train converted into heat. The glycol solution was continuously pumped through a radiator for cooling. As the hydro-kinetic brake was decreed unsuitable for slow speed application, a hydraulic operated friction brake assisted the hydro-kinetic system below 50mph.

With running a train at a higher maximum speed and decelerating at greater speed, while maintaining or even improving passenger comforts, gave additional work to the Research Division. Most problems were overcome by installing double glazing, improved sound insulation and air conditioning.

After all these areas of research had been delved into and satisfactory results obtained, all that was needed was project approval, which came in 1969. The way was then clear for Research to demonstrate its theories by the building of Advanced Passenger Train – Experimental.

When authorisation was given for the APT project, as well as construction of the train, the project covered the formation of the Old Dalby Test Track over part of the former Midland Railway route, as well as the building of an Advanced Projects Laboratory at the RTC, both of which are described in separate sections of this book.

Before construction of the APT-E train could commence, considerable research had to be undertaken into the tilt system and the proposed articulation bogie, and for this research an APT-POP (Advanced Passenger Train – Power-O-Power) was built. In its 'as built' form the 'train' consisted of two power car body shells sharing an APT-E style articulation bogie, with APT type power bogies/ modified articulation bogies at vehicle ends. The POP body shells were built by Metro-Cammell of Washwood Heath, Birmingham, and delivered to the new Advanced Projects Laboratory by road on 30th October 1970. The vehicles were of welded box sections formed as a space frame. The shells had a body mounted 'room' which contained the tilt and levelling power packs as well as a small surveillance area. Cab ends and body cladding were not provided as this was considered likely to inhibit the test programme. In its original form the train did not have operational brakes but was through piped – able to operate between laboratory or escort vehicles, which were specially fitted with compatible couplers. In later research programmes hydro-kinetic and friction brakes were added.

Whilst the body shells were under construction at Metro-Cammell, the bogies were assembled at Derby Locomotive Works. The original type fitted was three articulation bogies, consisting of a main longitudinal bolster which supported the vehicle which was attached to the bogie frame via a transverse bolster. The bogie frames were formed of two separate assemblies, each carrying a wheelset, the frames of which were able to yaw relative to each other, enabling the wheelsets to be steered to radial positions under control of rail/wheel guidance forces. The yawing of the frames was governed by dampers and swinging arms. The swinging arms also acted as anti-roll bars for the steering beam which formed a non-tilting base for the tilting suspension jacks. The tilt system 'picked up' lateral acceleration parallel to the floor and tilted the vehicle body. The acceleration was calculated by accelerometers, one mounted in the roof and the other under the floor of each vehicle. The measurements of the accelerometers were processed, along with the roll rate, to produce outputs to servo-valves controlling the hydraulic power packs which operated the vehicle tilt system to a maximum of 9 degrees. As safety was always of paramount importance, if a defect occurred in the tilt system the 'tilt' became passive – giving the vehicle normal suspension characteristics.

Throughout early 1971 the POP train was prepared in the Advanced Projects Laboratory at Derby, and by early September was complete for yard testing. The 'train' was transferred to the Old Dalby Test Track on 15th September. During the following week wheel and bogie observation tests were carried out, mainly at slow speed, traction being provided by the Research Division's 'Uni-mog' road/rail vehicle. After its initial bogie tests the POP train commenced exhaustive trials, firstly on the Old Dalby Test Track and latterly on the LM main line. This test programme continued throughout 1972/73 when the POP train, although in various revised forms, with different bogies, operated on the WCML mainly north of Crewe.

Before the POP train entered service the APT-E, had been ordered. The 4-coach 'unit' was to be formed of Power Car 1 (PC1), Trailer Car 1 (TC1), Trailer Car 2 (TC2), and Power Car 2 (PC2), and be assembled in the Advanced Projects Laboratory. The body shells were supplied from GEC Engineering of Accrington for the trailer cars, and Metro-Cammell for the power cars. The main purpose of building APT-E was to evaluate the suspension system and tilt equipment, and for this the set was built as a mobile instrumentation laboratory without significant passenger accommodation. When complete APT-E was 288ft 0^{1}/2in in length with power supplied by four Leyland Automotive gas-turbines in each power car, each driving a Houchin 400 Hz alternator. Each power car had a fifth identical turbine/alternator which provided 415 volts auxiliary power. The power cars used conventional diesel fuel which was carried in a 300 gal underslung tank, power car ventilation being provided by side louvres. The PC layout was arranged with a centre area, between traction and auxiliary power were hydraulic packs for suspension/brake.

The traction motors used on APT-E were conventional axle hung dc sets, and although this gave a higher than required unsprung mass this had to be accepted. The traction motors were geared to give a maximum speed of 195mph. Braking was provided by air supplemented by hydro-kinetic brakes in the 50-150mph range. Because of the choice of traction motors the bogie was an 'H' frame with two transverse members. The wheel diameter was 36in.

With the APT and the considerable increase in speed came the aerodynamic styling of the front end, but this still had to contain the driving position into which considerable research and detailed design effort was placed. The front ends of the power cars were specially strengthened to protect the driver with a hydraulic buffer ram mounted behind the front fairing. Also, a crumple-zone was positioned to the rear of the cab to 'fold up' in the event of heavy frontal impact. The cab itself was air conditioned and soundproofed, with the driver's position in the centre. A full description of the cab is given under the illustration.

The physical construction of APT-E was of aluminium alloy stressed skin, riveted to frame members, closely following previous aero industry practices.

As indicated prior, APT-E's role was as a mobile laboratory to put previous theories into an operational train – therefore TC2 was fitted as an instrumentation vehicle for monitoring the majority of the test functions. Facilities existed for up to 32 channels of data to be received at any one time; this was stored on magnetic tape for later analysis. Although only 32 channels were collected at any one time, the train contained the wiring for several hundreds of data receiving points. One interesting and novel feature of APT-E was the outward opening twin doors, which were situated in the car coupling module above the articulation bogies.

By Autumn 1971 APT-E was taking shape at the RTC, and during November it was painted in a very distinctive blue/silver livery and unveiled to the public by BR Board member (Engineering/Research) Mr Sidney Jones, on 16th December 1971, after which the seemingly endless task of equipment testing took place. It was not until 27th June 1972 that APT-E first ran under its own power. For several days trials were conducted in the yard of the RTC where many problems were identified, all of which were rectified by 6th July when static driver training commenced. By early July the date was set for the first main line run – 25th July. This target was met with the train performing one run at 25–50mph between Derby and Duffield.

Regrettably, following this successful run the train did not operate again for over a year due to a manning dispute with the drivers' union ASLEF. To enable the APT research programme to be continued TC1 was removed from the set and placed in the Research Division's Engineering Test Hall for extensive structural evaluation, while the power bogies were later transferred to the POP train, which was permitted to operate during the ASLEF 'blacking'. Results from these tests identified many modifications which were required, which were effected during the stand-down period. As the RTC was not geared for this remedial work the set in its 3-car form was manoeuvred to the nearby BREL Derby Locomotive Works on 16th November and placed in No. 7 Shop where it remained for the following eight months. Major modifications were carried out whilst at the Works, including alterations to the hydraulic packs, wheelslip detection modifications, the redesigning of certain electronics, rebuilding the articulation bogies, the installation of traction motor blowers, the reprofiling of the wheels, modifications to the turbines and structural alterations to body components such as the installation of seating, lounge and toilet facilities in TC2.

By April 1973 the ASLEF manning dispute was resolved and APT-E was again made ready for the road, departing from Derby Locomotive Works for the RTC on 27th June 1973. APT-E was transferred to the Research Test Track at Mickleover on 9th August for ten days basic testing and crew re-familiarisation. After 17th August APT-E was returned to the RTC for major testing to commence on 20th August. The first runs operated by the unit were as far as Leicester, which was followed by a trip to Beeston, and on these runs speeds of up to 90mph were recorded.

On 3rd September 1973 APT-E was transferred to the purpose-built Test Track at Old Dalby where testing was carried out. After a short period following the introduction of rheostatic braking, a traction motor bearing failure necessitated a wheelset being returned to Derby for attention. This was completed by 18th September when the set returned to testing and soon attained a new speed record for the train of 100mph. By late September much experience of the train was being gained and on 11th October a high speed run was undertaken where 128mph was attained. During the following week the decision was taken that before further high speed testing could be carried out the hydro-kinetic brakes had to be installed, the train returning to the RTC on 18th October. Modifications to the hydro-kinetic braking were completed on 26th November, the wheelsets were installed and testing recommenced on the Old Dalby line in early December, returning to the RTC for the Christmas period.

In January 1974 APT-E was again transferred to Old Dalby for hydro-kinetic brake evaluation, and this continued until late March when the set was returned to the RTC for a major 'update' programme. During this second update or 'stand-down' period, the Leyland automotive turbines were modified to give a total train output of 3,300hp. A major setback to the gas-turbine story came during the update period when Leyland announced it was withdrawing from the automotive turbine field. This announcement came at the same time as BR indicated that production APTs would have electric power. To enable the research programme of APT-E to continue Leyland agreed to provide a support programme for the train's prime movers until 1976.

During the course of the update period TC1, which had taken part in the structural research programme, was returned to the set and fitted with a small amount of seating.

By early July APT-E was recommissioned and again returned to Old Dalby for traction, brake and tilt testing, in the course of which, with the aid of the uprated turbines, a new record speed of 131mph was reached. In August a serious tilt problem was identified but this was eradicated by the power cars running passive for several months. Main line running for the first time to the south of Leicester took place on 28-30th August when the train worked to Cricklewood and back. In the weeks that followed many main line runs were carried out as well as trips on the Old Dalby line, culminating on 6th December when the 10,000 miles barrier of APT running was broken. By early 1975 APT-E was again back at Derby were extensive modifications to the tilt system were effected, with test running resuming in early March. On 17th March one of the most prestigious operations of APT-E to date occurred, when the set visited the London terminus of St. Pancras, and during the ensuing weeks operated a number of high speed runs between London and Derby.

Although the design speed for APT-E was 155mph, after two years of exhaustive trials the maximum speed achieved had been only 136mph. To correct this position the WR agreed to carry out high speed APT tests of up to 155mph on Sundays, 27th July, 3rd and 10th August 1975. For this three week period the home of APT and the Research team was Old Oak Common, with runs scheduled for several weekdays as well as the weekend test periods on the main line. Operation over 120mph was restricted to Sundays and then only between Reading and Swindon when the line was closed to normal service. The actual section of line authorised for the 150+mph speed testing was between Goring and Uffington. During the first few days on the WR several trials were operated between Old Oak Common and Swindon – not all without problems. The three Sundays of speed tests were carried out successfully with a maximum speed being recorded for the train on 10th August of 152.3mph. After APT-E's final run on 10th August the train returned to Derby.

For the remainder of August and most of September APT-E remained at Derby, where further research into the tilt system was undertaken which culminated in a two week period on the Old Dalby Test Track from 29th September. Also, preparation work was undertaken for high speed running during October on the Derby–St. Pancras route, where authorisation was given for 115mph operation. The St. Pancras–Derby runs were most successful and on 30th October a high speed dash between St. Pancras and Leicester was organised where the 99.1 miles were covered in a staggering 58 mins 30 secs, with a maximum speed of 136.9mph being recorded.

Little of great note came of APT-E after October as by now all resources were being deployed on the development of the electric prototype. However, during November and December APT-E was returned to the Old Dalby Test Track where a load measuring wheelset, which had been developed by BR Research over the past 36 months, was installed for wheel/rail force measurement. This, in contrast to the modern disc brake set previously installed, was a spoked wheel reminiscent of the steam age! Most of the load measuring tests were carried out on the curves at Upper Broughton and Folly Park. In early January 1976, APT-E still with its spoked wheel, operated several main line tests but until its final research run on 2nd April, spent most of its time at Old Dalby. On 2nd April 1976 the set returned to the RTC for the last time when the job of dismantling much of the instrumentation equipment commenced in preparation for the train's presentation to the National Railway Museum, York, which had shown a keen interest in having the set as an exhibit. On 11th June 1976 APT-E was moved under its own power to York and when it arrived had clocked up 23,559 miles of research service.

Of course, much of the data obtained from running APT-E was utilized in design and production of the APT prototype electric sets, especially in respect of the tilting suspension systems.

Whilst BR Research played a small role, such as effecting tests on the APT prototype, once the APT-E was taken out of service BR Research's involvement with the Advanced Passenger Train project was almost over as some 95% of APT-P work was undertaken by the M&EE Department.

BR Research into APT took another turn from 1974, when a pre-production APT-P body shell, built by BREL Litchurch Lane, was stress tested in the Engineering Test Hall and later coupled between the two POP cars. By now these were heavily modified with cladding and were mounted on independent bogies.

Other Research operations on the APT theme included the modification of a redundant Hastings Line buffet car as a tilt test coach which was mounted on two end trailer bogies, and as the vehicle was slightly narrower than conventional coaches, body tilting experiments could be carried out whilst remaining inside the loading gauge. Another vehicle adapted for APT tilt tests was 'Trestrol', No. RDB901603 which was used to test the anti-tilt pantograph suspension system.

One of the first items of APT hardware to take to the road was RDB511023 (HSFV1), a conflat vehicle fitted with weight packs and used for high speed curving tests. The modified suspension and wheelsets proved that speeds well in excess of 100mph were practical.

The first sign of active testing in conjunction with the APT development project was the operation of the POP train, formed of skeletal APT shaped vehicles mounted on APT bogies, to evaluate the tilt systems. The POP train is seen headed by the Division's Class 17 No. 8512 on 14th October 1971 at Edwalton, on the Old Dalby Test Track.

J. Hooke

Once the Advanced Projects Laboratory was complete and open, all APT vehicle work was concentrated in this building. Prior to the POP train becoming operational the APT-E power car shells were delivered by road from Metro-Cammell in Birmingham. The first of these (PC1) is seen inside the Advanced Projects Laboratory along with the POP skeleton vehicles.

BR

The body of APT-E was assembled in an aluminium alloy stressed skin, riveted to a skeleton frame, this closely following aerospace practice. The raw and empty shell of PC1 devoid of its nose cone is pictured in the Advanced Projects Laboratory.

BR

APT-E in complete form poses outside the Engineering Test Hall at the Railway Technical Centre on 24th July 1972, the day prior to its inaugural main line run. Note the missing valance cover on the nose end, showing the coupling access point.

The Late Brian Haresnape

APT-E takes its first steps on the main line on 25th July 1972, while returning from Duffield, after a highly successful test run. Little was it known when this picture was taken that APT-E would not operate on the main line again for over a year, due to a manning dispute.

Author's Collection

After settlement of APT-E's manning problems the set commenced testing and research running. APT-E is seen departing from St Pancras on 17th March 1975 with a return test special for Derby.

BR

To effect the huge amount of research required into tilting vehicles, one of the Division's laboratory cars, Lab 4 No. RDB975386 was mounted on modified APT tilting bogies for evaluation purposes. The vehicle was ideally suited to this research role as it was a former 'Hastings' profile coach, which would permit an amount of tilt prior to the vehicle becoming out of gauge. In addition to its APT bogies the coach was stripped of its conventional drawgear and installed with bar couplers. RDB975386 named *Hastings* is seen in the RTC yard during 1984.

From 1974 the APT 'POP' train was modified with an APT-P vehicle being built and formed between the original POP vehicles, which were re-mounted on revised bogies and given body cladding. The 3-vehicle set then performed bogie and ride research work, mainly on the West Coast Main Line. The pre-production APT-P car was allocated No. RDB975636 and identified as Laboratory 8 and named *Pilot*.

In addition to the APT research and development work the Advanced Projects Laboratory carried out several weeks of testing on the prototype HST power cars when delivered from BREL Crewe in June 1972. Car No. 41001 is illustrated inside the Vehicles Laboratory soon after arrival.

The Main Laboratories

The Vehicles Laboratory

This laboratory, constructed in 1968/70, was originally designed as the Advanced Projects Laboratory where APT theory could be transferred into reality. The laboratory building with rail access at the north end (two tracks) has a floor space of 16,200sq. ft. Towards the middle of the building is an elevated control tower which is soundproofed and air-conditioned. This building is conveniently positioned so that supervisory staff have good all round visibility of the operating area.

Apart from having the ability to accommodate two rail vehicles at the same time on roads installed with deep illuminated inspection pits and all the usual services, the laboratory has a number of specialized features. These include:

Roller Rig. Installed in a 200ft x 20ft pit, designed to take a full-sized vehicle and simulate speeds of up to 200mph, the rig equipment now consists of one shaft driven roller fitted with a brake. The main use of this rig was in suspension development and tilting tests for the APT project.

Brake Dynamometers. For research into braking systems two brake dynamometers are installed, the more modern and versatile of which consists of two main flywheel shafts connected by a right-angled spiral bevel gearbox, with a ratio of 1.8:1. The axle loads are simulated by varying the inertia or flywheel load, and the simulation of rising or falling gradients by use of drive motor torque up to a maximum of 1.25KNm. Under normal operation the dynamometer rotates up to 2,130rpm with a maximum test torque of 15KNm. The inertia available from the main shaft can be varied from a minimum of 300 Kg.m^2 to a maximum of 2400Kg.m^2, the alteration being adjustable in 50Kg.m^2 increments.

Wheels to be tested on the dynamometer can be up to 1.2m diameter and are mounted in a tailstock system. If required a gearbox can be installed at the end of the main or high-speed shaft which increases its output to 3,000rpm, the apparent inertia at the test wheel being cut by approximately 50%. On the secondary or low speed shaft a pair of rollers is provided onto which wheelsets can be installed. To simulate actual conditions the wheelsets are 'loaded' against the rollers to a maximum of 200KN. The axle load simulated by the inertia flywheel may be varied from 5 ton to 20.5 ton in steps of 0.45 ton.

Provisions are made on the rig to simulate poor conditions, ie wet or greasy rails. The dynamometer rig is designed to be used for single brake application tests, a series of repetitive applications or constant speed drag braking against a specified torque. All outputs from speed, torque, deceleration and braking time are recorded in the adjoining instrumentation tower where up to 32 channels of data can be collected at one time.

The Servo Hydraulic System. For the testing of vehicle suspension components and research into vehicle dynamics, a hydraulic power pack, powered by a 130Kw motor, supplying up to 270lit/min of oil at a pressure of 21mn/m

via a hydraulic ring main is provided. Eight servo controlled valves govern the various actuators. Full control of the actuators is from the elevated control tower which also provides instrumentation. For the testing of vehicle suspension systems the actuators are attached either to the vehicle body (to determine secondary suspension parameters) or to bogie frames for primary suspension investigation. The hydraulic actuators are attached in the vertical direction to investigate pitch and bounce, and laterally to excite lateral and yaw motions. The purpose of all these resonance tests is to determine the ratio of the measured displacement to an applied force. In addition to complete locomotives/vehicles the actuators can be used to test smaller suspension components such as dampers, suspension links, air springs and secondary suspension systems.

Engineering Test Hall

The largest and the original BR Research laboratory is the Engineering Test Hall. The building is 170ft long x 192ft wide and has a floor space of over 32,500sq ft, containing the main machine shop, vehicle preparation area and structural testing facilities. Adjoining the Engineering Test Hall are smaller laboratories and the quadrangle of Kelvin House.

Vehicle Preparation Area. This area, consisting of three lines (Nos 12–14 roads) is where most BR Research vehicles are modified for their various test functions. Facilities exist for vehicles to be removed from their bogies if required – normally by jacks, whilst overhead cranes are provided for other lifting operations. Deep illuminated inspection pits are provided as well as the usual range of engineering support facilities.

Structural Testing Area. This section of the laboratory contains a comprehensive range of equipment for static and fatigue testing of structures or components, and for fatigue and fracture research. A special emphasis is placed on trying to re-create actual service conditions. A vehicle test rig is provided to test coach or freight vehicle structures up to 82ft in length, and can apply an end compression of up to 400 tonnes at differing heights. Facilities are also provided to apply vertical, static/dynamic loading as a distributed vehicle loading up to a total of 600KN. Six adjustable portal frames are used for testing large components eg bogies or bridge sections up to 49ft 6ins x 32ft 6ins x 16ft 5ins, with a maximum load capacity of 8,000KN. Several different portable testing frames from 5ft x 6ft to 12ft x 16ft can be used in conjunction with a varied selection of actuators operating from the hydraulic main to provide either static or variable loading conditions. As well as the above structural equipment, a range of fatigue testing machines are installed for evaluation of components and specimens of various size.

Within the Engineering Test Hall there is a wide and varying range of workshop machine tools which assist in the general engineering function.

Track Laboratory

The Track Research Laboratory, with its associated Test Hall is operated by the Track Development team. The main Test Hall measures 180ft long by 30ft wide, and contains a full length of ballasted track on which a self-powered vehicle mounted on a single loaded axle is operated, with the ability to travel at a speed of 1.5 m/s. Axle loading can be varied between 6–40 tonnes depending on the research programme being undertaken. The laboratory is also equipped with ballast testing facilities enabling the material to be tested in compression and for its abrasive properties to be measured in a Deval wet attrition test.

The principal area of work undertaken in the Track Laboratory concerns new methods of track installation and maintenance.

Scientific Services

This section of the Research Division occupies the former LMS Research building on the opposite side of London Road to the Railway Technical Centre and consists of Faraday House and Hartley House.

Subjects dealt with by this section include: Health and safety, effluent treatment, drinking water sampling, procurement and quality control of BR's supplies, control of used oils in service and lubrications, fire technology, air pollution, traffic and dangerous goods, forensic science, cleaning, adhesives, batteries, optics, fluid filtration, surface coatings, polymers and many other items coming under contract services and supplies.

General view of the Research yard showing the Engineering Test Hall in the centre and part of the Vehicles Laboratory to the left. In the yard, Lab 26, Lab 20 and locomotive No. 97201 can be seen.

View of the Research yard showing Vehicle Laboratory (former Advanced Projects Laboratory) in the centre background. The side of the Engineering Test Hall can be seen on the right. Two generations of diesel unit are to be seen in the foreground with RDB975010 *Iris* in the centre, this being a 1956 built Derby single car, while on the right stands the new DCE 2-car Track Recording set, developed by Research and built within a Class 150 body shell.

View of the Engineering Test Hall whilst under construction, showing the main structural and fatigue testing area at the west side of the building, with the fatigue testing pit in the far corner. On the left is one of the portal frames which can be fitted with different compression actuators, depending on tests being conducted.

BR

The east side of the Engineering Test Hall is set aside for rail vehicle preparation, which can include complete rebuilding of vehicles if required. This rare view shows the Railbus prototype LEV 1 on the right, the MAG-LEV 'vehicle' in the centre background, an LRT Underground vehicle undergoing private party work, and the prototype pneumatic ballast injection machine (stoneblower). The V-Laser track ballast re-profiling machine is in the foreground.

BR

The interior of the Engineering Test Hall, vehicle preparation area, does at times look rather cluttered, especially when a scaffold surround is erected around the vehicle to provide safe access. Here we see the Mark III test car Lab 21 No. RDB977089, under conversion to a high speed brake test vehicle. During the rebuilding work alterations to the existing windows were made as were a number of internal alterations. On the adjacent road ballast cleaner No. DR76302 can be seen.

To establish the rigidity of new designs of multiple unit cab the Research Division has undertaken a series of non-destructive tests on pre-production designs utilizing facilities in the Engineering Test Hall. One of the cab 'mock-ups' is seen prior to testing.

The Vehicles Laboratory is fitted with a powerful servo-hydraulic main, used for the application of power-packs to vehicle bodies and components used in the research into vehicle dynamics. VDA No. 201000 is seen undergoing major suspension tests following the installation of the Taperlite suspension system.

BR

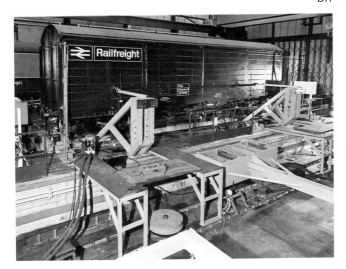

After the introduction of the Class 317 emus one set was temporarily allocated to the Research Division where major suspension, electrical and ride tests were carried out. This included the installation of complex electrical data collection equipment into the motor coach, No. M62670 as illustrated. Note the guard fence erected to protect staff.

Following the completion of the APT, the Advanced Projects Laboratory was used for a number of other research projects – including major suspension and dynamic force tests on locomotives and multiple unit vehicles. The hydraulic main is seen applying pressure to the front of a Class 507 DMS vehicle in this view.

Author's Collection

General view showing the interior of the Track Development Laboratory, with its own length of ballasted track and special vehicle which is propelled along the line for various track research tests.

There is a drop weight test rig, located on the opposite side of London Road to the RTC. The rig is used to test larger components such as rails, which are placed in the building at the bottom of the column. The rig has a 5 ton drop mass and a maximum drop height of 29ft 6in.

BR

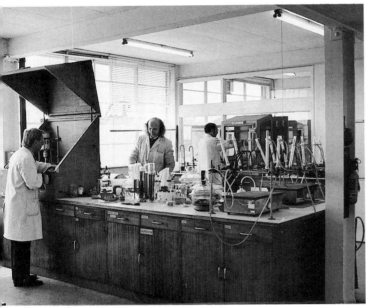

Two views taken inside the Scientific Services Section which occupies the original LMS buildings. The upper picture shows three scientists working in one of the laboratories while the lower one shows a Research display board to illustrate durability and repair of concrete structures.

Organisation and Management

Reference to the accompanying 'family tree' will demonstrate the basic organisation of BR Research with the Director of Engineering Development and Research being in overall control and answerable to the British Railways Board (BRB). Under that post comes the Director Research, responsible for the day to day running of the Research Division. In addition there is an Assistant Director (Research), and an Assistant Director (Development), together with Assistant Director (Programmes), and Assistant Director (Resources). Under this Executive Management comes the branches of Research, each being under a senior manager.

Towards the end of 1988 BR Research employed about 700 staff of which a high proportion have professional qualifications to graduate or equivalent level. Recruitment of staff is from within the railway industry as well as outside research organisations and universities, ensuring a continuing fresh approach which is matched by the experience of staff coming from traditional railway backgrounds.

During the mid-1980s there was considerable change in the financial support given to BR Research and the 1986/87 financial year was the first in which the Division was financed mainly by the railway business sectors. The influence of the business sectors, the BRB's procurement policy and the Rail Plan, have together led to widespread changes in role and relationships, which has not only affected BR Research but all technical functions. It has also become important to recognise the role of research in the overall process of the introduction of new technology, and establish the appropriate arrangements with the individual functions/sectors. Three key areas have therefore been established:

A.   The need to create a technical/business vision of the future on a 10–15 years timescale in order to determine the extent of the exploratory programme.
B.   The need to agree/review with the functions/sectors basic guidelines for the objective programme.
C.   The need to plan, and manage the skilled research manpower.

Research Relationship with the Business Sectors

With the everchanging field of the railway business sectors, periodic meetings between the Director of Engineering Development and Research, Director Research and the sector directors, has proved invaluable, assisting with short-term technical options for the business needs. Additionally the sector directors have become involved with some long-term projects such as the Advanced Multiple Unit (AMU) which has become the basis for the 'Networker' sets for Network SouthEast.

The Director, Engineering Development & Research, through the BRB's Research & Technical Committee, has instigated major technical policy studies involving specialist staff from BR Research, the technical functions and the business sectors. Findings from this group will assist in achieving agreed technical policies which will guide the appropriate research plans for the future.

In the recent past a closer relationship with the railway supply industry has been made, with a number of joint meetings with the Railway Industry Association (RIA) and major technical suppliers. These consultative meetings have provided the opportunity for a full discussion of the Board's plans and requirements for the future.

BR Research also has an active relationship with London Underground Ltd where exchange of research and development information takes place at regular intervals. The aim of this arrangement is to ensure that each organisation uses its resources effectively, avoiding duplication and establishing common development specifications.

The Research team also maintain contact with transport research organisations in Europe through regular exchange visits. BR Research also benefits through its membership of ORE – the Research Organisation of European and Overseas railways within the International Union of Railways (UIC).

Research Performance

During the course of each year a number of major projects move from the research phase into development and eventual implementation. In recent times this has included:

Multiple unit technology.
Rail straightening.
Trackside warnings.
Improved track components.
Solid State Interlocking (SSI).
Radio Electronic Token Block (RETB).
Automatic Route Setting (ARS).

During a recent typical year (1986/87) the BR Research team introduced eleven new projects into the objective programme, while in the exploratory field 20 projects were introduced. During the year Research produced 108 technical reports for internal BR circulation with a further 27 papers presented or published at national and international conferences or seminars. Additionally, 25 contracts were 'let' to universities or industry and 50 contracts awarded to BR Research from the private sector.

Funding

Funding for the Research Division consists of three elements. First a strategic exploratory research programme formulated and executed by the Research Division and funded by the BRB at a cost of £4 million. Secondly, an objective research programme formulated jointly by the Division, the Engineering functions and the business sectors, executed by the Research Division and funded by the business sectors at a cost of £5 million. Thirdly, a technical support programme solving problems arising in day to day operation is executed by the Research Division for the engineering functions and funded by the business sectors at a cost of £6 million. There is a separate programme costing £15 million carried out by the engineering functions in implementing the subsequent developments carried out by industry.

Research Tree

(December 1988)

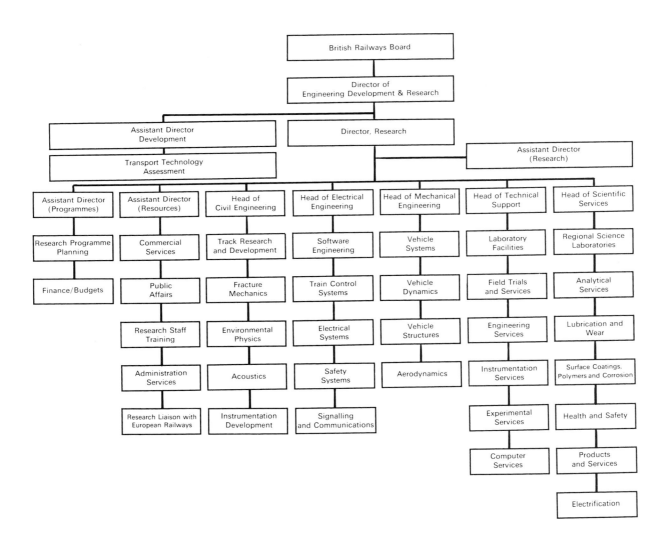

It should be noted that the Research programme is divided into two main categories.

1. **The Exploratory Research Programme:**
   A programme with strategic emphasis, examining technical feasibility and business potential at a conceptual stage before a secure role to implementation can be planned – development of core railway technology.

2. **The Objective Research Programme:**
   This heading covers the research phase of projects planned through development to implementation jointly with appropriate functions, sectors and the supply industry, including those which have grown out of the exploratory progamme.

Present and Future Projects Programme

At any one time the Research Division is planning and carrying out a significant number of independent research projects. Many of the past projects are well documented in this book while this section deals with some of the more important 'present' fields of research, as well as those broadly covered by the 1988–89 research programme.

During the course of the 1988/89 financial year the following breakdown of financial expenditure was awarded to the various elements of research, and this basic trend is projected for the foreseeable future.

Exploratory research	25%
Objective research	27%
Support for technical dept.	44%
Private party contracts	4%

1. Technical Policy Studies

This field of research began in the 1986 financial year to appraise future signalling policy options for both secondary and main lines. Two separate studies were authorised, one for secondary routes and one for main lines. The secondary route study was to investigate the applications of new signalling technology and to introduce cost-effective renewals on some lines – including the evaluation of further RETB installations. The main line study concluded that an evolutionary development from lineside signalling was the most favourable financially, but recognised that in selected areas a case could be made for a form of cab signalling and automatic train protection.

2. New Signalling and Control Systems

This programme builds on earlier work aimed at introducing cost-efficient micro-electronics and computer technologies into signalling fields. The major input to this is the Integrated Electronic Control Centre (IECC) which was due to be first installed at Liverpool Street for commissioning in Spring 1989. Other areas to benefit at an early stage from IECC being York, Newcastle and Yoker. Much further research is planned on signalling and control centres to keep abreast of this rapidly advancing technology. It is also projected to further advance Automatic Route Setting (ARS) with proposals for second generation equipment. During 1988 a feasibility review was authorised into the technical and economic possibility of using space satellite communications for railway applications.

3. Techniques to Aid Vehicle Specifications

This area of research aims to provide the 'tools' for ensuring that new vehicle specifications will result in lower life costs. It includes structural analysis, computer aids, modelling of vehicle dynamics, crash worthiness. A major effort is applied to multiple unit technology and to methods of improving control and braking. It includes work on the conceptional approach to high speed passenger vehicles. Special sections of this programme include investigations into novel brakes and establishing design principles for selected types, with the aim of operating beyond the 140mph barrier. Special research into the basic laws governing wheel/rail adhesion under various conditions of controlled wheel slip are to be carried out, as are ways of alleviating specific problems caused by poor control of traction and braking.

4. Improved Performance/Reliability of Traction and Rolling Stock

This broad title covers a number of separate research functions, with many items of an objective nature being for the DM&EE. The main areas of work under this group consists:

Bainitic Wheels to increase disc braked wheel life through reducing thermally-produced wheel tread damage.

Dewirement Dynamics – identifying combinations of conditions under which dewirement of 25kV electric locomotives occur and improve design to reduce damage.

Improved Pantograph Head Material – research into new head strip material to improve wear and life costs.

Wheel Profile Research – development by computer prediction.

Friction Brake (Hot-Spot) Research – effected in an attempt to extend permissible power and energy absorption limits of conventional brake configurations by reducing thermal stresses.

Diesel Engine Monitoring (DEMON) – this research project installed on Class 37/5s Nos 37506 and 37512, was devised to investigate the application of traction system monitoring equipment.

High Performance Brake Development – project to demonstrate the durability of off axle brake equipment, including the hydro-kinetic and gearbox brake systems.

Leafguards – Establishing rules for the design and cost effectiveness of leafguards for SR emu stock.

Weld Repairs of Wheels – investigate the possibilities and cost savings of repairing wheels by welding.

Transmission Retarder – research how road industry style retarders might be developed for use on dmu stock.

5. Improved Methods of Track Maintenance and Renewals

Under this heading many separate fields of research are again grouped, the main areas being:

Track substructure; Improved land usage by earth reinforcing; Void detection in tunnels and bridges; Track condition monitoring – to investigate the feasibility of providing vehicle mounted equipment capable of monitoring track conditions; Prevention of deterioration of concrete structures; Research into deterioration of masonry structures; Tunnel repair methods; Ballast cleaning methods; Welding of rails; Final development of new rail flaw detection train; Improved track alignment techniques; Embankment and cutting slope stability; Research into conversion of jointed track into continuous welded rail; Switch and crossing maintenance reliability; Rail life extension.

6. Customer Services

Research involved in technical/business system studies and passenger information systems derived from signalling data form the main area of investigation. One of the first applications of the research designed Computer Aided Timetable Enquiry (CATE) system of passenger information assistance has been commissioned at a number of telephone enquiry bureaux in Network SouthEast including Waterloo.

7. Maintenance and Improvement of Technical Productivity

The maintenance of specialist knowledge in Railway Technology remains the core of this work. Main headings identified for research include: Passenger comfort studies – to measure objectively passenger reaction to vehicle ride, and to develop computer calculations which will enable the DCE to assess the comfort level of any type of vehicle on any type of track; Fundamentals of noise generation of rail vehicles on rails; Fundamentals of ground-borne vibration; Improve fatigue life techniques; Research and design new train performance programme.

Although externally looking like any other Class 37/5s, Thornaby allocated Nos 37506 *British Steel Skinningrove,* and 37512 *Thornaby Demon* are testbeds for a Diesel Engine MONitoring system. This includes a micro-processor which receives information from many parts of the locomotive and provides a read-out on their condition upon request. The second locomotive to have the DEMON equipment, No. 37506 is seen inside the Vehicles Laboratory during fitting out.

The use of radio equipment on the railway has developed considerably in recent years. First with the introduction of RETB (Radio Electronic Token Block) and more recently the NRN (National Radio Network) and cab – signalbox communication systems. Much of the ground research on these schemes has been performed by Test Coach *Iris* which is equipped with radio signal surveillance equipment. The upper view shows No. RDB975010 *Iris* at Guildford whilst carrying out signal surveillance work in conjunction with the Waterloo area train – signalbox communication system. The lower view shows the inside of the coach which contains special equipment for signal strength pickup and recording.

The Research Division recently carried out a major project for the Director of Civil Engineering, with development of a new track recording unit. Research's involvement began in mid-1987 when a 2-car body shell conforming to the Class 150/0 standard was delivered from BREL York. The set was then fitted out with sophisticated equipment and handed over to the DCE on 3rd November 1987, and is seen here in the Research yard.

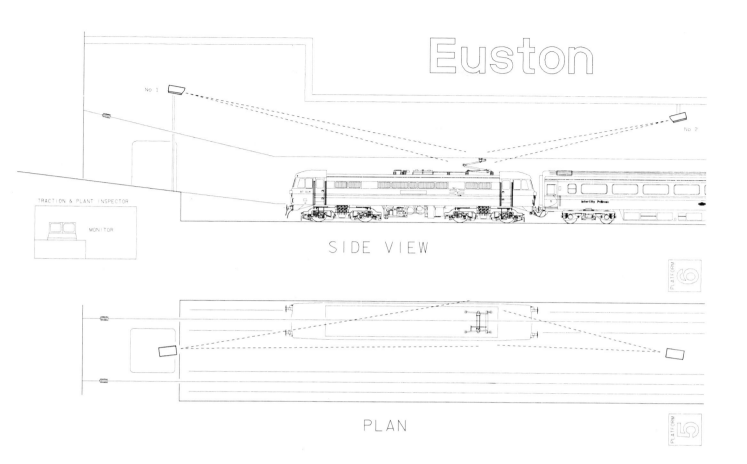

SIDE VIEW

PLAN

To assist in locating damaged or defective pantograph pick-up heads, Research, in conjunction with industry, have erected a television based monitoring system at Euston, where video cameras can be trained on pantographs to inspect their condition. The monitor for the equipment is housed in a nearby office.

BR

A vast amount of work has been placed on the development and use of electronics in signalling, culminating in the building of an operational central Integrated Electronic Control Centre work station within the RTC to demonstrate the ability of the system. This will also serve to iron out any problems before the IECC system is installed at Liverpool Street. This view shows the RTC signalling work station.

BR

During recent years much research has been carried out into the further development of containerised freight transport. This has included the development of a Maxilink and Minilink container for the Railfreight Speedlink sub-sector, with easy transfer from road to rail vehicle, without the use of terminal equipment. Each container is built with its own set of legs to enable easy storage and conforms to conventional lifting practices for rail wagon mounting. Containers of two different sizes have been constructed. These two views show a container supported by its own legs and mounted on the rear of a Speedlink distribution wagon.

Author/Michael J. Collins

One of the areas of research is tribology, investigating the science of adhesion on rails. For this research the Division operates a 3-vehicle formation: RDB975046, RDB999900 and RDB975076, of which RDB999900 is fitted with wheel slip/slide simulation equipment and independently controlled brake packs. Motive power for the train is normally provided from within the Research organisation. The Trib train powered by now withdrawn Class 97/2 No. 97201, is illustrated at Old Dalby.

RDB999900 was a specially built COV-AB constructed to Research requirements and fitted with end corridor connections and a large amount of internal test equipment. The upper view shows the vehicle in the Trib train consists, while the lower plate shows one of the wheelsets surrounded by various control items. Note the legends on the bodyside indicating 'no brakes', and warning that the test brakes controlled from an attached Laboratory may be activated at any time.

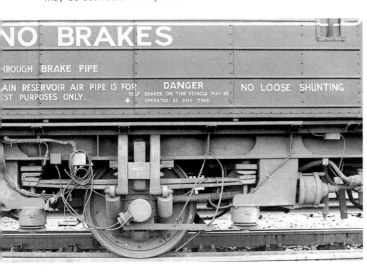

Mickleover Test Track

What is now known as the Mickleover Test Track was formerly a section of the Great Northern cross-country route from Grantham to Nottingham and Stafford, which was partly joint with the North Stafford Railway. The route was opened on 1st April 1878, continuing in use by both passenger and freight traffic until 4th December 1939, when the section between Derby Friargate and Egginton Junction closed to passenger traffic. The route did, however, remain open for infrequent freight traffic until 3rd February 1964, when the section westward from Mickleover to Egginton Junction was closed and made available to the Director of Research as a test track. Later in the year the Train Control Group moved to a site adjacent to Mickleover station. Hitherto this group had occupied accommodation at Derby Friargate station.

For use by BR Research some, comparatively minor, alterations were carried out at both ends of the $5\frac{1}{4}$ mile line. At Mickleover a two-road single-ended shed, 150ft in length was built. When assembled the shed was fitted with all the usual mains supplies as well as a 60 amp power connection and a deep, illuminated inspection pit was installed in one road. Sufficient accommodation inside the shed existed for four vehicles. To the rear of the shed in the former station yard, staff accommodation was built, this comprised a small laboratory area, messing facilities, workshop and control room. To the side of the shed a concrete apron was provided where limited lifting and storage was possible. This area was additionally fitted with a small container lifting frame used in conjunction with auto-wagon experiments in 1971, when the Train Control Group demonstrated the technical feasibility of automatically controlling a single container vehicle utilizing a self-propelled wagon.

The line from Mickleover to Egginton Junction was formerly a two track section, however Research retained only one through line from the Mickleover end, with a second track remaining for some four miles to assist with test train movements and ancillary testing. The additional track was lifted in 1988.

As previously indicated this line was originally intended for the occupancy of the Train Control Group, and for their purposes inductive track loops and a number of lineside control cabinets were provided throughout the line.

Within the test track a variety of different track types, ie bullhead rail on timber sleepers, flat bottom rail on timber and concrete sleepers, continuous welded rail on concrete sleepers and a section of paved track were installed, to evaluate vehicle track interaction with differing rail conditions. Facilities also existed within these different track types to impose irregularities, such as a hump or dip in a single or pair of rail joints or lateral misalignment. These deliberate defects could be introduced to enable vehicle ride response to differing track features to be determined.

In more recent years, the Mickleover Test Track has been used for a variety of tests including the Tribology Train and test running for the M&EE Section of new generation dmu stock.

During the mid-1980s when BR Research were keen to expand their knowledge within the field of aerodynamics, a purpose-built aerodynamics test facility was erected on the site of the former down line, opposite Mickleover train shed. The construction of this facility was carried out in 1985/86 and consists of a 457ft 6in long x 9ft 9in semi-tubular housing formed of a metal frame, skinned in white nylon sheeting, with a thick netting for added safety. Inside, a 1/25th scale double track model railway was built, elevated for easy access. Model trains can be propelled along the tracks at speeds of up to 125mph. Propulsion for the laboratory trains is provided by a 'catapult' which fires the train along the line via an underslung acceleration trolley. Braking is effected by the model engaging a retarder, and to safeguard against any unforeseen failures in this area a foam cushion is provided at the end of the track. To ensure complete safety during high speed operations, no person is permitted inside the housing when tests are in progress, control being effected from a Control Centre which has closed circuit TV coverage of the facility. Data from the test runs is either recorded in the adjacent Control Centre or in an instrumentation vehicle berthed alongside.

It is anticipated that the aerodynamic facility will assist engineers to solve the many such problems associated with trains running at high speeds, especially those travelling in tunnels. Investigations are currently being conducted into the nature of unsteady air flows in tunnels, aerodynamic drag, transient pressures, air-flow velocities and thermal effects. It is hoped that the rig will prove to be a valuable design aid for aerodynamic aspects of the Channel Tunnel, particularly in relation to the basic tunnel configuration and rolling stock design.

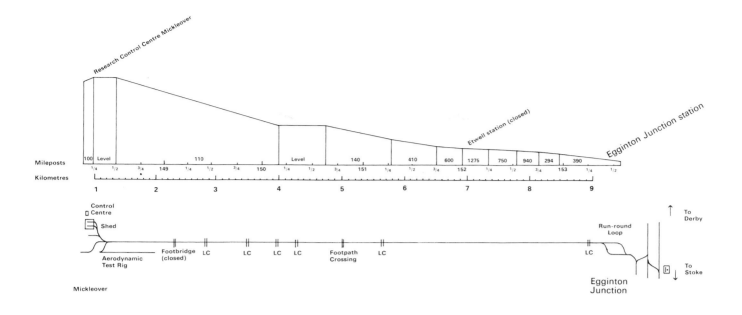

Mileposts

Kilometres

Control Centre

Shed

Aerodynamic Test Rig

Footbridge (closed)

LC   LC   LC   LC

Footpath Crossing

LC

LC

Run-round Loop

To Derby

To Stoke

Egginton Junction

Mickleover

On a few occasions enthusiasts' specials have been permitted to travel over the Egginton Junction – Mickleover line, one such occasion being 28th March 1987 when the "Mickleover Hypothesis" operated, formed of Class 115 stock. The train is seen here passing the old station at Egginton Junction.

John Tuffs

View of the Research Division Mickleover site looking south, showing the recently introduced Aerodynamic Test Laboratory on the right. This building is constructed from a steel tube framing with a reinforced plastic cover. On the left of the illustration is Lab Coach 15 *Argus* which was being used to record data from the aerodynamic rig.

General view of the Mickleover site looking from the Egginton Junction direction. On the left is the recently constructed aerodynamics facility, while on the right the 2-track train shed can be seen. The wiring in the tracks in the foreground is the remains of a previous research project involving track/train communication.

In addition to Research operations the Mickleover Test Track is used for some M&EE Department tests, including new dmu types. On 25th February 1985 Metro-Cammell prototype No. 151001 is seen being propelled by Class 31 No. 31327 at Etwall during ride performance tests.

John Tuffs

View inside the Aerodynamic Laboratory, showing the test track on the left and walkway to the right. To conform with the very stringent health and safety requirements, when the rig is in operation, no person is permitted inside the Lab, all operations being overseen from an adjacent control room which is equipped with closed circuit television.

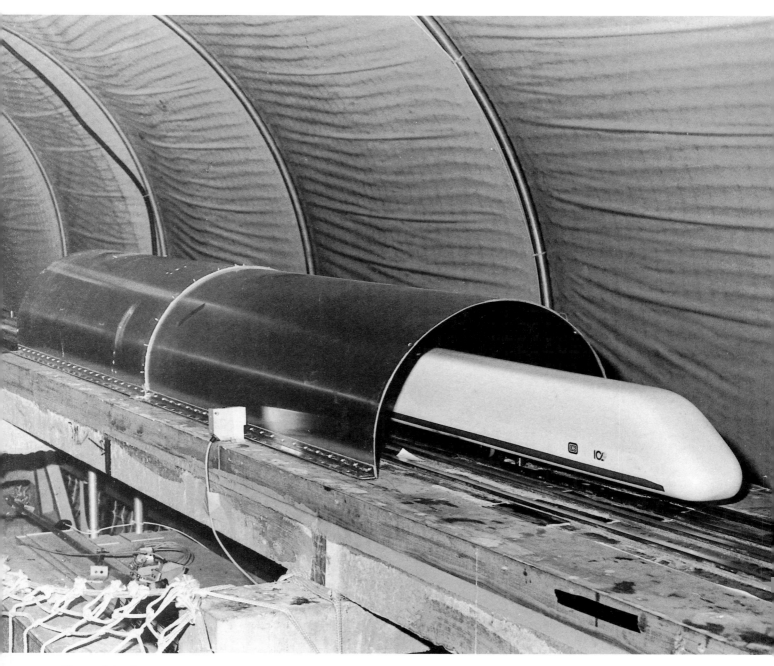

The model trains catapulted along the aerodynamic rig can travel at speeds of up to 125mph. To determine the aerodynamic forces generated with the train passing different line-side features, such as tunnels or bridges, various items can be introduced which are fitted with instrumentation equipment. This view of the track shows a model based on the DB ICE high speed electric train emerging from one of the removable tunnel sections.

As with all Research installations, security is essential. At Mickleover a private security company provides the required cover, complete with guard dog to deter any unwelcome guests.

View showing the Mickleover 'Research' line diverging from the main line at Egginton Junction. In the distance, on the right is the former station building, now occupied by a construction firm.

John Tuffs

Old Dalby Test Track

Included in the APT-E investment was sufficient finance to convert and commission an Advanced Passenger Train test track – where research, development and testing of full sized vehicles could be undertaken at up to design speed.

The line provided for the project was a 13¾ mile section of the former Midland Railway Nottingham-Kettering line between Melton Junction (Melton Mowbray) and Edwalton, which was closed to normal traffic from 1st May 1967.

The route – as shown in the accompanying diagram – was ideal for the projected test operations, although major modernisation was needed before testing could commence. BR Research drew up plans and work was effected by the Divisional Civil Engineer, Nottingham, who handed the track over to the Director, Research, in 1969.

The track was designed for testing APT-E at speeds up to 155mph (with canting), and conventional stock at speeds of up to 90mph. One of the design objectives was to produce a section of line which was maintained to a general standard rather than to artificial test levels. A mixture of wooden and concrete sleepers was incorporated as well as differing types of rail, point and crossing.

From Melton Junction, where all trains entered the line, a single line lead headed onto the test track via Holwell Sidings, which ran parallel with the test track for a short distance. Just prior to Asfordby Tunnel is the test track arrester bed which is the final 1/8th mile of the test track, and is enclosed by steel sheeting and filled with eurathene, which, if impacted by a train, would slow and stop the vehicle/locomotive without causing serious damage. The single test track then continues at a steady climb towards Saxelby Tunnel en route passing the run-round facility for the Melton end of the line, the line then continues to the summit of Grimston covered way before descending at 1:212 through Grimston Tunnel and towards the line's control centre and yard at Old Dalby.

The Old Dalby site, purpose-built for its research role, consists of a single lead off the test track into a gated compound. Inside the compound a short siding is provided which ends just prior to the workshop building, the main siding continuing through the double-ended workshop. The workshop itself is fitted with a drop wheel pit and an overhead crane. Adjacent to the workshop is the Old Dalby Control Centre, office and amenity block, together with fuel storage facilities. A run-round loop is provided within the siding area which has another siding leading off it, which has been used for track buckling experiments. After Old Dalby the line continues downgrade to milepost 112, before climbing and curving towards the site of Upper Broughton station, where the route then drops downgrade again, curving for a further 1¼ miles before commencing the long straight section through Widmerpool station and on to Stanton Tunnel. This has the former second track retained for ancillary testing for its entire length. After the tunnel exit the route continues downgrade through Plumtree to the run-round point at Edwalton. A few hundred yards past the run-round a further arrester bed is positioned.

During the course of the APT-E trials on the line, BR Research decided to erect a two mile section of overhead catenary, but this was not energised but was for use on pantograph experiments. The catenary supporting masts were positioned at half normal spacing and the catenary system scaled as far as tensions and weight were concerned. Travelling from north to south along the line the following sections were encountered:

A. Half tension length of full scale Channel Tunnel style equipment, including a section of heavy compound equipment.
B. Half tension length of full scale MkIII catenary.
C. Full tension length of scaled MkIIIA equipment.
D. Full tension length of scaled stitched equipment with equal spans and rigid droppers for dynamic experiments.
E. Half tension length of MkI compound equipment.
F. Half tension length of full scale MkIII equipment.
(This equipment was retained after conclusion of APT operations.)

Within the three mile straight section facilities were incorporated to introduce depressions in one or both rails at joints to produce the dipped rail joint effect. Widmerpool station retained one of its platforms which had its surface raised to conventional height, principally for aerodynamic experiments. Facilities also exist on the platform for small laboratory work.

Following the completion of the APT research operation, the line has remained the property of BR Research and has been used for numerous test programmes involving either laboratory or service stock. On a number of occasions the line has been used by the M&EE section for vehicle evaluation, including pantograph and riding tests with Classes 89, 90 and 91 electric locomotives.

On 17th July 1984 the Old Dalby site was used to stage the spectacular CEGB nuclear flask collision when Class 46 No. 46009 was driven (without a driver) at nearly 100mph into a pre-positioned nuclear flask, laid across the tracks. The collision was carried out to dispel fears that if a flask was involved in a rail accident it would not stand up to the impact. However the collision, in front of hundreds of press and photographers, proved that the design of the rail flask was totally successful.

It is anticipated that the Old Dalby Test Track will be retained for at least the foreseeable future and play a role in a number of projected research operations involving traction and rolling stock.

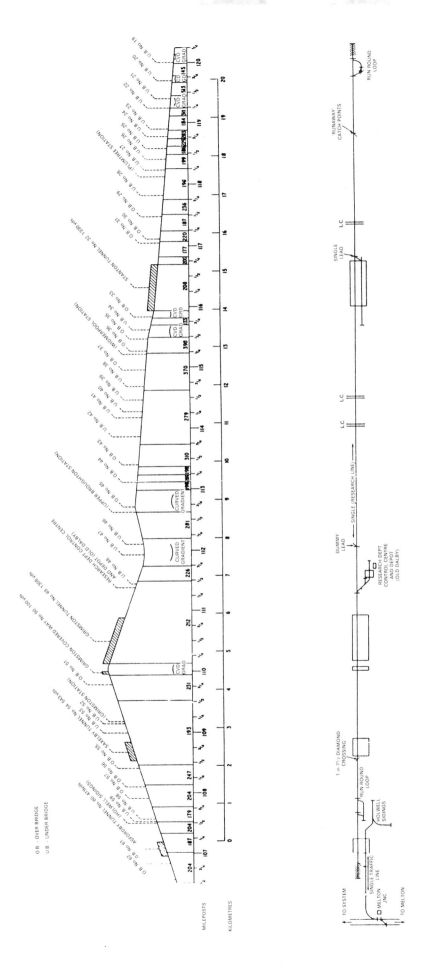

**Melton Junction – Edwalton Line
Research Department Test Track Layout**

O B – OVER BRIDGE
U B – UNDER BRIDGE

Although the second and larger of the two Research test tracks extends from Melton Junction to Edwalton, most of the active testing is concentrated on the section between Old Dalby and Edwalton. Parked on the (single line) test track adjacent to Old Dalby, we see the Trib train with the 'Auto Trailer' leading.

General view of the Old Dalby Control Centre. The workshop is on the right – able to accommodate one vehicle, and the office amenity block is to the left. When this illustration was taken Railbus LEV1 was under evaluation.

BR

For the entire 1,340yd long Stanton Tunnel the second track has been retained for ancillary testing. The upper view shows the Research Division's Leyland Experimental Vehicle 1 (LEV1) performing one of its first research runs in 1979, about to enter the tunnel. The lower picture, taken some 18 months later, shows the Research modified 'Stoneblower' track machine posing for a photograph. By virtue of its pleasant surroundings, Stanton Tunnel has been used for a number of official photographs.

Both: BR

A two mile section of the Old Dalby Test Track is equipped with overhead catenary. This is not energised and was originally erected for APT pantograph development, six different styles of overhead power line being provided. In this illustration we see 'flat top' No. RDB787319 or HSFV4 stabled under the catenary, while in the distance rail pack vehicle No. HSFV1 can be seen.

BR

As previously mentioned, the Old Dalby line was heavily used for APT-E development work, where straight, curved and gradient tracks could be encountered, ideal for high speed tilt tests. APT-E is seen at high speed with a full 9° cant to the left near Broughton.

BR

of Security.

View of the staged CEGB 'collision' at Old Dalby on 17th July 1984, when withdrawn Class 46 No. 46009 was crashed into a pre-positioned (empty) nuclear flask to prove that they could withstand the force of such a collision. The illustration shows the scene some three seconds after impact. Note the flask-carrying vehicle can be seen flying through the air in the centre of the picture.

Research Main Line Testing

Whilst much of the Research Department's work is carried out at the main Derby base, together with rail-borne experiments performed on the Division's test tracks, a significant number of test trains (about 550 a year, split 290 Test Track and 260 purely main line) operate over BR revenue-earning lines.

When it is necessary to operate test trains over running lines the Research Division liaise closely with the relevant Regional Operations Manager with regard to train times, crews and where applicable, motive power.

When a research team carries out 'test' or 'trial' operations away from the Railway Technical Centre they normally involve using one or several of the Division's vehicles, which, depending on the work to be undertaken, may occasionally be supplemented by 'traffic' vehicles.

All preparation, including modifications to locomotives would be carried out in either the Engineering Test Hall or Vehicles Laboratory and marshalled in a train consist in the Research yard, where thorough testing is carried out prior to authorisation being given for main line running.

When carrying out active tests the train is manned by several Research personnel who are responsible for monitoring the performance of the technical equipment on the train. This is carried out under the supervision of a technical officer. The overall running of each test train is placed with the officer in charge of tests, whose primary duties are to liaise with the train crew, the operators and to ensure safety at all times.

When trains are on BR running lines all test trains are manned by drivers and guards from a local depot, who are accompanied by a regional traction inspector.

The accompanying illustrations show a varied selection of test trains in operation on BR running lines that incorporate Research Division vehicles.

In the early years of wheel/rail interaction 'Trib' research the 3-vehicle Trib Train travelled some 14,000 miles in one 12-month programme alone. Motive power was provided by a locomotive from the revenue fleet, this being prior to the Division receiving dedicated motive power. Here, Class 25 No. D7560 traverses the Midland Main Line north of Loughborough hauling the original Trib set. The data collection COV-AB No. RDB999900 is in the centre.

BR

Following transfer of "Baby Deltic" No. D5901 to the Research fleet in 1970, this locomotive became stable power for the Trib train for several years. Carrying the Research route indicator – 1Txx, No. D5901 approaches Wolverhampton High Level on 6th October 1972 with a Derby RTC – Derby RTC via Birmingham, Crewe, Uttoxeter special.

Geoffrey Bannister

After allocation of the redundant Class 24 No. 24061 to the Research Division – where it was originally numbered RDB968007, this locomotive became the normal Trib train motive power, as well as being used for other research operations. The locomotive remained in normal service albeit numbered 97201, until withdrawn at the end of 1987. One of the more geographically adventurous outings undertaken by the Class 24 and the Trib train was on 15th November 1976 when the entire formation was operated to Plymouth for wheel/rail adhesion tests over the Devon banks. The train is seen at Dawlish Warren.

David Nicholas

Instrumentation for the Trib train is provided by a fully equipped laboratory coach No. RDB975046 (Lab 11) which is always attached to the Trib test vehicle when in operation. The former seating compartments of this redundant BSK now house computerised data collection and recording equipment, as well as many different control modules for the Trib brake slip/slide units.

The 2-car Laboratory 5 set, used for track recording using inertial measuring equipment has traversed virtually the entire rail network since its introduction to Research Division stock. These two views depict the unit in action, the top illustration showing the set near Duffield on 17th April 1984 while en route to the Railway Technical Centre. The lower picture shows the set near Treeton Junction, Sheffield, during a track recording run of Sheffield area freight lines in July 1975.

John Tuffs/Les Nixon

In recent years one of the most prolific 'active' Research Division trains has been Test Coach *Iris* No. RDB975010, which has travelled to virtually all corners of the railway network to evaluate radio signal strength for various projects as previously mentioned. For these changing duties different methods of signal pick-up have been fitted. The upper illustration shows *Iris* wth a large nose-mounted plate aerial, while the lower photograph shows *Iris* at Dorking working on the SR driver only operation radio system, where the pick-up was received via a roof mounted aerial.

When in operation *Iris* is normally staffed by a three man research team, with a driver being provided by the most convenient local depot with dmmu traction knowledge. *Iris* is seen approaching Effingham Junction in March 1988, with a DOO signal strength special from Selhurst.

Brian Morrison

Research were widely involved in the design, development and testing of 'Railbus' theories, which were pursued in an attempt to provide alternative low-cost rural transport. The first item of Railbus hardware was Leyland Experimental Vehicle 1 (LEV1) which was assembled by Research with components supplied by Leyland Bus. LEV1, allocated Research No. RDB975874, is seen at Ipswich while operating passenger evaluation specials on the Lowestoft line.

Michael J. Collins

One of the few occasions that passengers have had the opportunity of travelling on Research allocated stock was during November 1981 when Railbus No. RDB977020 was used on passenger service on the Bristol-Severn Beach line. On 10th November the vehicle is seen departing from Redland with the 10.08 Bristol-Severn Beach.

A two vehicle research train formed of RDB975000 (Lab 1) and RDB602150 (Lab 25) named *Decapod* is seen departing from Crewe during track testing on 19th July 1983. *Decapod*, a rebuilt Freightliner flat, is fitted with an additional centre wheelset which applies and records lateral and vertical forces of the rail.

John Tuffs

Following the completion of service trials the prototype IC125 or Class 252 set was returned to the M&EE Department at Derby where the set was disbanded. The power cars were both taken into M&EE stock as 'tractor' power for test trains, (mainly involving APT-P work), while some of the trailer vehicles passed to Research, some to M&EE and others were rebuilt for Class 253 use. On 21st November 1980 one of the prototype power cars hauls Research Lab 1 No. RDB975000 and a Class 252 trailer vehicle past Normanton-on-Soar bound for the Old Dalby Test Track.

John Tuffs

An unusual formation photographed on 27th July 1987 of Research Class 97/2 No. 97201 seen passing Kegworth on the Midland Main Line, hauling former Manchester/Sheffield/Wath line Drewry Car No. RDB998901 en route from Old Dalby to the Railway Technical Centre. The 'Drewry' Car is not through brake fitted, and the 20 tons goods brakevan was accordingly attached to the rear and a speed restriction of 25mph imposed.

John Tuffs

If Research requires to operate tests on a mainline, the route between Derby-Leicester/Bedford or Cricklewood is often used. In conjunction with bogie development the test train illustrated was operated on 18th May 1984 formed of Class 31 No. 31296 hauling Lab 12, bogie bolster No. B945972 and Lab 10. On this occasion the train was working between Derby and Leicester and is seen passing Cossington.

The most modern of the Research owned test vehicles is *Argus* which has been used on a number of main line testing programmes. In the summer of 1988 Lab 15 was used for the testing of Class 91s, being based at Bounds Green. *Argus* is seen in Research stock consist after returning to Derby.

Test coach *Mercury*, rebuilt in 1973 from a BCK, was used as an instrumentation vehicle for the Train Control Group. Internally the coach was converted to provide a generator compartment, staff accommodation and data collection area. One of the first major projects undertaken by *Mercury* was transponder research, investigating methods of track/train communication, and it is seen at Euston.

BR

In a further attempt at introducing low-cost replacement coaching stock, research in conjunction with the M&EE, mounted a modified Leyland bus body on a former MkI underframe. After initial RTC testing the coach, still carrying its Research number RDB977091, was put into normal passenger service on selected cross-country duties to gauge passenger opinion as well as provide active testing. The coach is seen at Banbury formed in the 10.23 Manchester-Brighton of 7th October 1983. This project was later abandoned.

John Tuffs

Another research transit move recorded on film is this taken on 4th May 1975 at Clay Mills, near Burton, of Class 31/1 No. 31124, heading a Derby Research Yard-Old Oak Common train, conveying Lab 10 No. RDB975428 and M&EE Test Car No. 10, No. ADB975814.

John Tuffs

Hydra – the hydraulic traction fitted single car – RDB975385 was used on a number of active tests after conversion in 1974, in an attempt to design a novel hydraulic transmission system. *Hydra* was tested on the Midland Main Line as well on the Research test tracks. This view shows the vehicle in its early days, with only one hydraulic bogie fitted, subsequently both bogies were fitted for hydraulic operation and the vehicle operated many thousands of miles.

BR

For the testing of line and vehicle electrical systems the Electrical Systems Section operate Lab. Coach 6 *Prometheus,* which is a converted MkI BSK mounted on BT10 bogies, giving a maximum speed of 125mph. This side elevation of *Prometheus* shows the lower roof section able to accommodate a pantograph on the left. Note that the vehicle inscription indicates that the home base is Rugby.

BR

Research Division Stock (Complete List)

(Vehicles in bold are currently in service.)

Number	Type Code	Name	Lab No.	To Stock	Former Number	Description	Brake Type	Notes
Locomotives								
D818				1973	D818	Spares for No. D832.	Vacuum	Kept at Swindon
D832				1973	D832	Track development dead weight vehicle.	Vacuum	Non active
15705				1968	D5705	Traction unit.	Vacuum	Also No. RDB968006.
D5901				1970	D5901	Traction unit.	Vacuum	
RDB7076				1973	D7076	Track development dead weight vehicle.	Vacuum	Non active.
RDB7096				1973	D7096	Track development dead weight vehicle.	Vacuum	Non active.
S18521				1970	D8521	Spares for No. D8598.	Vacuum	Non active.
D8598				1972	D8598	Traction unit.	Dual/EP	
97201		Experiment		1975	24061	Traction unit.	Vacuum	Also No. RDB968007.
97203				1987	31298	Traction unit.	Vacuum	
97204				**1987**	31326	**Traction unit.**	**Dual**	
97403		Ixion		**1984**	46035	**Traction and adhesion test locomotive.**	**Dual**	
97404				**1984**	46045	**Spares for No. 97403.**	**Dual**	**Non active.**
97472				**1988**	47472	**RTC (Research) Motive Power.**	**Dual**	
97480				**1988**	47480	**RTC (Research) Motive Power.**	**Dual**	
97545				**1988**	47545	**RTC (Research) Motive Power.**	**Dual**	
97561				**1988**	47561	**RTC (Research) Motive Power.**	**Dual**	
97801		Pluto		1978	08267	Remote control test locomotive.	Vacuum	Also No. RDB968020.
Locomotive-hauled ex-passenger/NPCCS vehicles								
RDM395840	QXV		26	1964	M9025M	Rail flaw probe guidance system.	Vacuum	
RDM395984	QXV			1975	–	Turbine test coach/workshop.	Vacuum	Also No TT45.
RDB975000	QXA		1	**1970**	M1003	**Vehicle dynamics test coach.**	**Air**	**Max. speed 125mph.**
RDB975001	QXV		2	1970	M1004	Stores vehicle.	Vacuum	
RDB975002	QXA		3	**1970**	M1005	**Instrumentation vehicle.**	**Air**	**Max. speed 125mph.**
RDB975036	QXV		22	**1971**	W9234	**Track maintenance vehicle, V-laser**	**Vacuum**	
RDB975046	QXX		11	**1970**	M34249	**Vehicle/track interaction test coach.**	**Dual**	**Tribometer train.**
RDB975076	QXX			**1971**	E34500	**'Auto Trailer' for vehicle/track interaction.**	**Dual**	**Tribometer train.**
RBD975081	QXX	Hermes	17	1971	M35313	Driving Trailer vehicle – instrumentation.	Dual/EP	Now with DCE
RDB975117	QXV		7	1971	M34319	APT development vehicle – electrics.	Vacuum	
RDB975136	QXX		12	**1972**	E34505	**Acoustics tests**	**Dual**	
RDB975146	QXO			1971	S15239	Air conditioning/Fire tests.	Hand	Non active.
RDB975266	QXV			1972	E70478	Stores vehicle.	Vacuum	
RDB975278	QXV		15	1972	W3082	APT kitchen car mock-up.	Vacuum	
RDB975280	QXX	Mercury	18	1973	S21263	Instrumentation vehicle – C-APT.	Dual/EP	Now with DCE
RDB975294	QXV		8	1973	E4453	APT interior mock-up.	Vacuum	
RDB975311	QXV			**1973**	S423S	**Equipment carrier – generator.**	**Hand**	
RDB975420	QXV			1974	M34144	Track test vehicle.	Vacuum	
RDB975421	QXO		13	1975	M34068	Aerodynamics/wind louvre test rig.	Hand	Non active.
RDB975422	QXB	Prometheus	6	**1975**	W34875	**Electrical systems test coach.**	**Air/TVP**	
RDB975425	QXV			1976	M34454	Aerodynamic test vehicle.	Vacuum	
RDB975427	QXX	Wren	14	1975	M323E	Acoustics test vehicle.	Dual	
RDB975428	QXX		10	**1975**	M9236	**Match vehicle.**	**Dual**	
RDB975429	QXV			1975	M15903	Stores unit – track development.	Vacuum	
RDB975547	QXB		23	**1976**	M81617	**Match vehicle.**	**Air/TVP**	**Max. speed 125mph.**
RDB975606	QXA	Electra	2	1976	S3068	Rapid Transit bogie test vehicle (TAIM).	Air	
RDB975667	QRV			**1978**	M37210	**Track maintenance equipment vehicle.**	**Vacuum**	**Former CCT.**
RDB975792	QRV			1978	E1322E	Track maintenance vehicle.	Vacuum	Former CCT.
RDB975793	QRV			**1978**	E1329E	**Generator vehicle.**	**Vacuum**	**For LAB 22.**
RDB975956	QRO	Phoenix	7	**1980**	M35061	**Fire test vehicle.**	**Hand**	
RDB975983	QXO			1980	M12162	Fire test mock-up vehicle.	Hand	
RDB975984	QXA	Argus	15	**1986**	W40000	**High speed instrumentation vehicle.**	**Air**	**Former IC125 car.**
RDB977089	QXA		21	**1986**	W40500	**High speed brake/suspension test vehicle.**	**Air**	**Former IC125 car.**
RDB977091	QXA			1982	E21234	Leyland 'Bus' body MkI.	Air	
RDB977468	QXA			**1988**	M5169	**Research support vehicle.**	**Air**	
RDB977469	QXA			**1988**	M5190	**Research support vehicle.**	**Air**	
RDB977470	QXA			**1988**	M5134	**Research support vehicle.**	**Air**	
RDB977525	QXA			**1987**	E19476	**Test train riding vehicle.**	**Air**	
RDB977527	QXA			**1987**	Sc48204	**Tilt testing vehicle.**	**Air**	**Former APT car.**
RDB977530	QXA			**1987**	W19481	**Dead weight coach for brake tests.**	**Air**	
Multiple Unit Vehicles (ex revenue)								
RDB975003	QWA	Gemini	16	1966	Sc79998	Train Control test unit.	Air	Battery power.
RDB975004	QWA	Gemini	16	1966	Sc79999	Train Control test unit.	Air	Battery power.
RDB975010	QWV	Iris	19	**1967**	M79900	**Train control radio test vehicle.**	**Vacuum**	
RDB975018	QWV		21	1968	M79047	Linear motor test unit.	Vacuum	
RDB975019	QWV		21	1968	M79053	Linear motor test unit.	Vacuum	
RDB975089	QWV		5	**1970**	M50396	**Track instrumentation unit.**	**Vacuum**	**TRIM train.**
RDB975090	QWV		5	**1970**	M56162	**Track instrumentation unit**	**Vacuum**	**TRIM train.**
RDB975385	QWV	Hydra	9	1974	M55997	Hydraulic transmission/braking development.	Hydraulic	
RDB975386	QXA	Hastings	4	**1974**	S60750	**Suspension and tilt test vehicle.**	**Air**	
RDB975813	QWA			**1988**	43001	**Dead weight test vehicle.**	**Air**	**Former IC125 MB**
RDB975964	QXO			1980	E59466	Fire hazard test vehicle.	Hand	
RDB975993	QXO			1980	E59458	Fire hazard test vehicle.	Hand	
RDB977225	QWV			1984	Sc52014	Test unit.	Vacuum	Not introduced.
RDB977226	QWV			1984	Sc59787	Test unit.	Vacuum	Not introduced.
RDB977227	QWV			1984	Sc52032	Test unit.	Vacuum	Not introduced.
RDB977842	QWV			**1988**	M53475	**Coach washing test vehicle.**	**Vacuum**	
–	QWV			1975	Sc56464	Instrumentation vehicle.	Vacuum	Returned to ScR.
–	QWV			1975	E56071	Instrumentation vehicle.	Vacuum	Returned to ER.

Purpose-built Single Unit Diesel vehicles

Number				Old No.	Description	Brake	Notes
RDB975874				LEV1	Experimental lightweight 'Railbus'.	Air	
RDB977020		Sold to NIR		LEV3	Experimental lightweight 'Railbus'.	Air	
RDB999507			20	None	**Wickham self propelled lab vehicle.**	**Air**	

Locomotive-Hauled freight stock (ex revenue)

Number	Code	Name	No.	Old No.	Description	Brake	Notes
RDW17901	ZXO			W17901	Van for stores.	Hand	
RDW87208	ZXV			W87208	SPV/fish van – generator.	Vacuum	
RDW160207	YXO			W160207	'Warflat' sleeper loading.	Hand	Max. 35mph.
RDW161021	**YXO**			**W161021**	**'Warflat' vibrator test vehicle.**	**Hand**	
RDE181322	STV			E181322	Track stabilisation vehicle.	Vacuum	
RDE262310	ZXV			E262310	'Vanfit' stores.	Vacuum	
RDE278491	**ZXV**			**E278491**	**'Lowmac' stores vehicle.**	**Vacuum**	
RDE284758	ZXV			E284758	'Vanfit' stores.	Vacuum	
RDM461074	**ZXV**			**M461074**	**Rail buckling winch wagon.**	**Vacuum**	
RDM478649	**ZXV**			**M478649**	**Rail buckling winch wagon.**	**Vacuum**	
RDB602150	**YXA**	*Decapod*	25	**B602150**	**Lateral track loading vehicle.**	**Air**	
RDB602548	YXA			B602548	Cross-braced bogie vehicle.	Air	
RDB753305	ZXV			B753305	'Vanfit' stores.	Vacuum	
RDB781568	ZXV			B781568	'Vanfit' – instrumentation.	Vacuum	
RDB787319	**ZXX**			**B787319**	**Vehicle/track interaction stores vehicle.**	**Dual**	Also No. HSFV 4.
RDB901401	YXO			B901401	'Protrol' (Rail store).	Hand	
RDB901600	YXO	*Atlas*		B901600	'Trestrol EC' Track measuring vehicle.	Hand	
RDB901601	YXO	*Cyclops*		B901601	'Trestrol EC' Track measuring vehicle.	Hand	Max. 35mph.
RDB901603	YXA		24	B901603	'Trestrol EC' APT bogie test vehicle.	Air	
RDB904651	YXO			B904651	'Lowmac' lateral pull vehicle.	Hand	
RDB904698	**YXV**			**B904698**	**'Lowmac' stores vehicle 'Mag-Lev' transporter.**	**Vacuum**	Max. 45mph.
RDC921000	**YXA**			**DC921000**	**100tonne Steel. LTF bogie tests.**	**Air**	Max. 85mph.
RDB945972	YXR			B945972	'Bogie Bolster' – LTE bogie test rig.	Piped	
RDB948407	**YXV**			**B948407**	**'Boplate' stores vehicle.**	**Vacuum**	
RDB951634	CAV			B951634	Brake van.	Vacuum	
RDB998546	**YXA**			**B998546**	**'Convex' Freightliner tests.**	**Air**	
RDB999091	ZXV			B999091	Tank wagon – storage.	Vacuum	

Purpose-built freight stock

Number	Code	Old No.	Description	Brake	Notes
RDC460000	ZXR	–	Structure gauging vehicle 'Optical Car'.	Piped	
RDB511023	**ZXB**	–	**Track/Vehicle interaction test vehicle.**	**Air**	Also No. HSFV 1.
RDB999900	**ZXR**	–	**COV-AB 'Tribometer' test vehicle.**	**Special**	Max. 90mph.

Internal user vehicles – Research Division allocated

Number	Old No.	Description	Brake	Notes
024296	A6090	**4-wheel 45T Shell oil tank.**	Hand	Also No. RDB6090.
024497	W94507	**Fire test section workshop/store.**	Hand	Non active.

Miscellaneous Stock

Number	Name	No.	Old No.	Description	Brake	Notes
RDB975634	*POP*		PC3	APT suspension development vehicle.	Piped/air	
RDB975635	*POP*		PC4	APT suspension development vehicle.	Piped/air	
RDB975636	*Pilot*	8	–	APT suspension development vehicle – intermediate TC	Air	
RDB965344				**Unimog road-rail vehicle.**		Reg. No. DRC 730J
RDB998900	**ZWO**			**Drewry Car OHLM inspection vehicle.**	Hand	Spares for No. 998901.
RDB998901	**ZWB**			**Drewry Car OHLM inspection vehicle.**	**Air**	
MAG-LEV				Magnetic-Levitation test vehicle.	Linear	
APT-E				Advanced Passenger Train – Experimental. (PC1, TC1, TC2 and PC2)	Air/HK	4-car set.

Track Machines

Number	Old No.	Description	Notes
DB96	74407	**Track development section tamper.**	
RDW7258	DW7258	**Ballast injection machine.**	TOPS No. DR73116.
DX73110		06-16-CTM spares machine.	
DX73112		06-16-CTM spares machine.	
RDB3956	B30W	Wickham trolley (site tests).	
RDB965279	DB965279	Stone blower tests.	TOPS No DX75039
RDB965454	TT54	'African Queen' Measuring system tamper.	
RDB966045		Track maintenance machine RTC.	

Research Department Road Vehicles

Number	Description
FDN 96S	Mini Bus – site vehicle.
YCH 903M	Road Lab for Train Control Group.
XNU 995Y	**Minibus for Track Development Group.**
PCH 623R	Scammell Routeman for container transfer tests.
JCH 369K	**Road Lab for Field Trials Section.**

BR Capital Fleet Vehicles used by Research Division

Number	Code	Description
B201081	VDA	Brake test actuation vehicle.
B601050	FGA	Minicon container wagon tests.
B462740	RBA	Match wagon for Freightliner wagon (Minicon trials).

D832. After withdrawal 'Warship' Class 42 No. D832 *Onslaught* became the property of the Research Division where it was used as a dead weight locomotive in conjunction with permanent way deformation experiments on the Old Dalby research line. After its Departmental career ended No. D832 was stored at Derby and later Egginton Junction before being saved from the breaker's yard by enthusiasts. The locomotive is seen in the company of Nos D7096, D8521, and D7076 at Egginton Junction on 21st May 1977.

Geoffrey D. Griffiths

S15705. One of the first allocated items of traction to the Research Division was Metro-Vic Co-Bo No. D5705, which was handed to the division after withdrawal in December 1968. No. D5705 renumbered to S15705 was used on the Tribology test train, as well as on general Research train movements. The locomotive is seen shunting back into the RTC yard.

P.J. Garrington

D5901 To provide dedicated traction power to the Research Division "Baby Deltic" No. D5901 was taken into Research stock in December 1969 and used on a variety of test trains, including the Tribology test unit. No. D5901 was superseded as Research power in November 1975 and subsequently broken up at Doncaster Works.

I. Lyall

D7076 and D7096. Two redundant 'Hymek' locomotives Nos D7076 and D7096 were obtained by Research after withdrawal, again for use as 'dead weight' vehicles in conjunction with track research. With bodywork in a deteriorated state No. D7096 is illustrated at Old Dalby.

D8598. After withdrawal from revenue service 'Clayton' Type 1 No. D8598 was taken over by Research as traction power for the Research Division's test trains. Few modifications were effected for its Departmental role and the livery applied was standard rail blue with full yellow ends.

EXPERIMENT

Nameplate *Experiment* as carried by Research locomotive No. 97201. The name *Experiment* was given to locomotive No. 97201 by the depot staff at Toton, who also gave the locomotive a classified overhaul and repaint in the early 1980s.

97201. To enable the Research Division to be more self supportive in terms of motive power, redundant Class 24 No. 24061 was transferred to Research use from 1975. Little modification work was carried out except for the fitting of a loco-train communication system. When first allocated to Research the locomotive was numbered RDB968007 and it is in this form that we see the locomotive alongside a former Class 252 power car at Derby 'E' shed in 1976.

After the adoption of the Research red/blue livery as standard, the former Class 24, by now carrying the No. 97201, was used on a variety of Research trains until the end of 1987. In the mid-1980s the locomotive was loaned for a number of Open Days, including the Diesel Weekend at the Midland Railway Centre on 12/13th July 1986, when the locomotive was used to haul special enthusiast services. The locomotive is seen departing from Butterley.

RDB975428 Lab 10. A vehicle extensively rebuilt for its Research role was No. RDB975428, modified from MkI BSO No. 9236. The former luggage cage was fitted with a large generator, while instrumentation was installed into the former seating bays. The saloon end of the vehicle was equipped with a driver's style observation window, and the end bodywork painted in yellow. The vehicle is mounted on B4 bogies and has a maximum speed of 100mph, and is currently used to control traction equipments on test locomotive *Ixion*. The first view shows the vehicle in Research blue/red livery, while the second shows the recently applied grey/red livery.

RDB975547 Lab 23. The only former BG to operate in the Research fleet is No. 81617 now Lab 23, which is classified as a Research train generator and match vehicle. Although having no on-board instrumentation, it is often wired for experiments with data being fed back to an attached instrumentation car. Research blue/red livery, with full yellow ends is applied. The presence of B4 disc-braked bogies permit a maximum speed of 125mph.

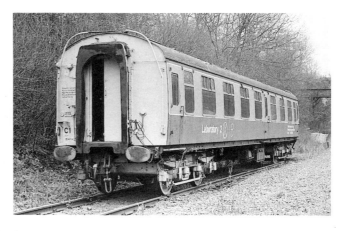

RDB975606 Lab 2. One of the Research vehicles that at the time of writing was awaiting disposal was RDB975606 a former MkI TSO, taken into Research stock in 1976. The vehicle was extensively modified for its Research career, having heavy current equipment installed to control experimental TAIM bogies. These two views show the vehicle painted in blue/red livery in store at Mickleover in Autumn 1987.

RDB975667. Former LMS Covered Carriage Truck (CCT) No. M37210, now forms part of the 3-vehicle track development train, being used as a stores vehicle. Few modifications have been carried out for its Departmental role. The livery currently applied is Research grey/red.

RDB975793. This vehicle was taken into Research stock in 1978 and was a former ER 4-wheel van. Today the vehicle is converted to a generator coach for Laboratory 22, for which purpose side louvres are positioned on both sides of the bodywork. The end of the vehicle coupled to Laboratory 22 is fitted with a gangway to provide staff access en route. The livery currently applied is Research grey/red.

RDB975956 Lab 7 *Phoenix*. Lab 7 *Phoenix* is used as a fire test facility operated by the Research Division's Scientific Services Branch. This vehicle, rebuilt from a BSK in 1980, is painted in the Division's blue/red livery and kept at the rear of Hartley House, adjacent to the Research Division's Drop Weight Test Rig. Although this vehicle remains on the active fleet it is not permitted on the main line – note the chimney on the roof!

RDB975984 Lab 15 *Argus*. The most modern, and by far the most sophisticated Laboratory coach operated by Research, is Lab 15 *Argus*, rebuilt from a redundant prototype IC125 buffet car No. W40000. *Argus* is operated by the Field Trials Section and is equipped with all the latest 'state of the art' computer based data collection and storage systems. Provision is made for the vehicle to collect up to 64 channels of data simultaneously from an attached vehicle or outside source. The two illustrations show *Argus* stabled at Mickleover, being used to collect data from the aerodynamic rig alongside.

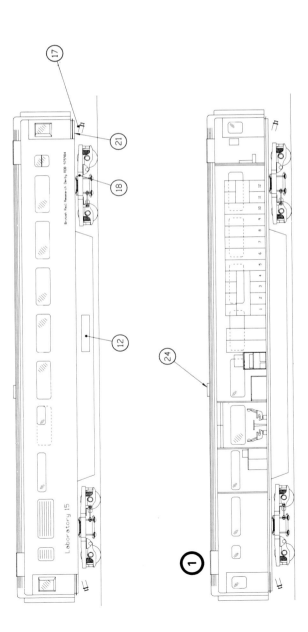

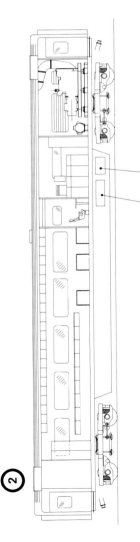

General Arrangement of RDB975984 *Argus*

1. 'A' side layout
2. 'B' side layout
3. Generator/alternator group
4. Instrumentation trunking
5. Fire and protective system
6. Kitchen area
7. Main structural partition
8. Instrumentation racks 1
9. Instrumentation racks 2
10. Worktop tables
11. Emergency equipment
12. Air conditioning module
13. Vestibule
14. Propelling equipment box
15. Light/heat control box
16. Toilet
17. Warning horns
18. AWS pick up equipment
19. Fuel tank
20. Underskirt store
21. Main entrance doors (4)
22. Body end doors
23. Coupling (Bar/Buck-eye)
24. NRN radio aerial

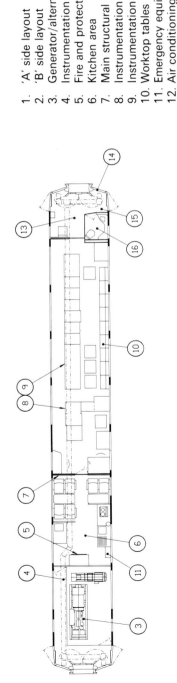

RDB977089 Lab 21. This former Class 252 prototype IC125 buffet car is now used as a high performance brake test vehicle. During 1988 major modification work was in progress and when completed provided the vehicle with three different braking types, including two wheelsets with a hydro-kinetic retardation system. Laboratory 21 is seen inside the Vehicles Lab in late 1987.

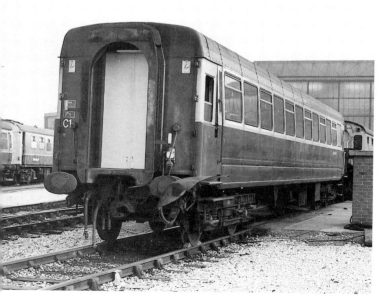

RDB977091. Research effected a project in the early 1980s in an attempt to introduce a low-cost replacement for the ageing fleet of MkI vehicles. One option Research exploited was the mounting of a heavily modified Leyland bus body on a redundant MkI chassis. However it was not popular with the travelling public with the consequence that the project was not pursued. No. RDB977091 is seen in the Research Yard.

RDB977525. After a lapse of several years Research started to acquire further vehicles in 1987. One of these was a former MkIIb TSO No. 19476 which arrived at Derby at the end of the year and is seen in this illustration awaiting conversion to a Laboratory vehicle.

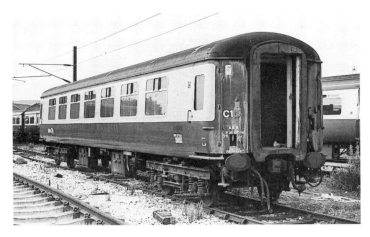

RDB977527. Following the termination of the APT-P project, car No. SC48204 was transferred to Research stock for possible future conversion to a tilt test coach. This vehicle was previously converted by Research for the DM&EE from an articulated coach to one with independent bogies. This view shows the coach stabled in the RTC yard.

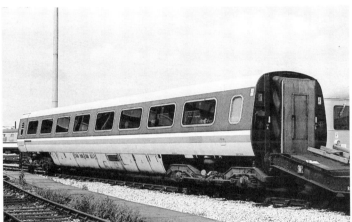

RDB975003 and RDB975004. This former 2-car battery powered set was one of the first unit formations to be obtained by Research, and used for 'BRATO' or British Rail Automatic Train Operation tests, using track/train mounted equipment. The set, numbered RDB975003 and RDB975004 was usually based at Mickleover and operated on the Mickleover – Egginton Junction line. It was painted in Departmental red/blue livery and after withdrawal has been preserved.

BR

RDB975010 Lab 19 Test Coach *Iris*. A very suitable vehicle for Research use is the single coach dmmu car – a self contained powered vehicle. BR Derby-built No. M79900 introduced in 1956 was acquired by the Division in 1967 as a mobile laboratory. Some rebuilding took place for its new role, namely the removal of the yellow diamond control system and installation of blue square driving controls. Internally the vehicle is set out with its laboratory function in the centre with staff accommodation at one end and a brakevan/generator compartment at the other. *Iris* is used for radio signal surveillance work and has been used in the development of the RETB system, driver/signalbox communication systems and the formation of the National Radio Network. The first illustration of *Iris* shows the vehicle in its BR traffic days at Buckingham after arrival from Bletchley on 27th June 1964. The two lower pictures show *Iris* in its present guise from the generator end.

J.N. Faulkner/Author/Michael J. Collins

RDB975018 and RDB975019. The research into linear rail vehicle propulsion reached the stage of an operational prototype in the early 1970s in the form of withdrawn first generation Metro-Cammell cars Nos 79047 and 79053 which were internally rebuilt to accept the linear system. To test the twin-car set a section of track equipment was installed on part of the Mickleover Test Track where many trial runs were conducted under the auspices of the Train Control Group. The livery of the set was BR blue with full yellow warning ends.

BR

RDB975089 and RDB975090 'TRIM'. This 2-car Park Royal built unit is operated by the Instrumentation Development Unit, and used for Track Recording by Inertial Measuring, hence the unit's identification as 'TRIM'. One coach of the twin set is retained for data collection and instrumentation purposes, while the other is a support coach, housing staff facilities. This set has operated to virtually all parts of the railway network, but is now scheduled for replacement. The livery applied is Research red/blue with side legends and numbers applied in white.

Author/Graham Scott-Lowe

RDB975385 Lab 9 *Hydra*. In 1974 the Research Division launched a project into the application of advanced hydraulic power for diesel multiple unit vehicles. To provide a testbed one bogie on former single car No. M55997 was hydraulic powered and evaluated both at the Railway Technical Centre, Derby, and on the Research test tracks. *Hydra,* painted in Research blue/red is seen at the Technical Centre in the upper illustration, while the lower picture shows the bogie detail which was based on the B4 type.

Both: BR

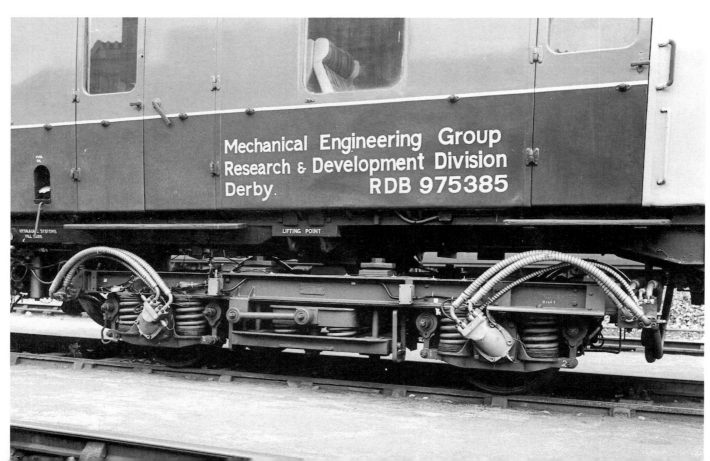

RDB975386 Lab 4 Hastings. Rebuilt from a Hastings line demu buffet car, *Hastings* was acquired by the Division for experiments into tilting vehicle suspension. The choice of this narrow bodied vehicle was made as a high level of cant could be introduced without the vehicle going out of gauge. Extensive rebuilding was carried out to this coach for its Departmental role, including the repositioning and alterations to windows, making end observation windows and, of course, installing sophisticated electronic measuring equipment. One end of *Hastings* is fitted with a bar coupler which necessitates the use of match wagons for general movement. Until late 1987 the vehicle was painted in the Division's blue/red livery, but now displays the Sector's grey/red scheme and is devoid of its *Hastings* name.

(Top) John Tuffs

RDB975874 LEVI. In the railway's quest to introduce new low-cost rural transport the Railbus was born. The first railbus to emerge was Leyland Experimental Vehicle 1 (LEV1). Assembled by Research in 1979 from bus body components supplied by British Leyland, which were mounted on a fixed 4-wheel chassis, LEV1 was, after completion, the subject of extensive structural and active testing before being placed in passenger carrying service – mainly in East Anglia. The livery of LEV1 was beige-yellow with full yellow ends. The above, left illustration shows the vehicle with a mesh windscreen protector installed prior to demonstrations in the USA. The view on the right shows LEV1 at Derby.

(Left) BR

RDB977020 R3. Many lessons were learnt from the construction and evaluation of LEV1, and with much new knowledge available BR/Leyland produced R3, assembled to Research requirements by BREL at Litchurch Lane from body parts of two Leyland National '2' single deck bus bodies. After post construction trials conducted by both Research and M&EE, No. RDB977020 was put into passenger duty on the Bristol-Severn Beach line and was later sold to the NIR. The upper view shows No RDB977020 at Litchurch Lane when new, while the lower view shows the vehicle on display at Laira. Note that a full yellow warning end was later applied.

(Above) BR

RDB999507 Lab 20. Built by D. Wickham & Co, this vehicle was assembled especially for Civil Engineer's track assessment and when new was provided with curvature, cant and point measuring equipment supplied by Elliott Brothers Ltd. Traction for the 'Railcar' was provided by a 97hp Meadows engine. After its CCE career ended in 1970, the vehicle became the property of Research and continued as a track measuring machine. When built No. 999507 was painted in brown/green livery; after take-over by Research blue livery was applied, which gave way to Research blue/red in 1986. These three views show the vehicle in all its various liveries.

(Above, left) BR

RDW160207. This 1943 GWR built 'Warflat' entered Research use in the late 1960s, being used by the Track Development Unit for sleeper/rail loading, in conjunction with vehicle/track interaction. This wagon was withdrawn in October 1985 and sold for scrap.

RDW161021. Another GW 'Warflat' to see Research service was No. RDW161021, taken into stock during the early 1970s and used as a track vibration vehicle, for which use an underslung slipper was fitted which applied vibration forces to the track. To provide power for the vibration unit No. RDW161021 was usually attached to generator vehicle No. RDB975311. To provide body weight for No. RDW161021 rail packs were mounted above the bogies. These two views show No. RDW161021 at Mickleover and illustrate both ends of the vehicle.

RDE278491. This vehicle is retained in stock to provide mobile storage facilities at the RTC or to transfer bulky equipment between Derby and the test sites. It is a vacuum fitted 'Lowmac', painted in Departmental green livery. The illustration shows the vehicle carrying a Class 455 cab section which has been the subject of non-destructive testing, to establish frontal deformation in cases of collision.

RDM478649/RDB461074. Two ex-revenue open wagons Nos DM478649 and DB461074 were taken over by Research in the early 1970s and converted to rail buckling winch wagons, used for imposing track deformations in conjunction with track development research. The two winch wagons are stabled out of use at Old Dalby and are unlikely to see further use. The livery applied to both vehicles is mid-yellow.

RDB602150 Decapod Lab 25. This unusual looking vehicle was constructed in 1967 as a Freightliner flat, but taken over by the Research Division in the early 1970s when extensive rebuilding took place; this included the fitting of a central laboratory area, weight packs over the wheelsets, power generation plant, messing facilities and guards accommodation. The 'vehicle' is used for lateral track loading and operated by the Vehicle Dynamics Group. To collect data a special retractable wheelset is mounted under the middle of the vehicle. *Decapod* is painted in Research blue/red livery and usually operates in conjunction with other laboratory vehicles. The upper view shows *Decapod* at the Railway Technical Centre, while the lower plate is taken at Crewe during WCML track testing.

(Below) John Tuffs

RDB787319 HSFV4. Another of the more unusual Research vehicles is No. RDB787319, a converted ferry van which was acquired by Research for modification and research into High Speed Freight Vehicles. After being handed to Research the vehicle was rebuilt at Derby with a 'flat top'. Originally the vehicle was painted in blue/red livery, but today it is grey/red, and operated by the Vehicle Dynamics Group and used for stores, being seldom seen on the main line.

RDB901601 *Cyclops*. Looking more like something from out of space than a railway vehicle is *Cyclops*, a modified Trestrol EC which was, until the autumn of 1987, used for track measuring operations under the auspices of the Track Development Unit. The research modification of this vehicle consisted of fixing a box-like structure onto the Trestrol, which was internally fitted with a generator, laboratory and staff accommodation area. For much of its life, when not in use, this vehicle was stabled on the northern section of the ECML. These two views show *Cyclops* after withdrawal at Mickleover. When initially designed this vehicle was to have laser measuring equipment (hence the name *Cyclops* – the one eyed monster), this equipment never being installed.

RBD901603. In conjunction with APT power collection research the Division rebuilt Trestrol EC No. B901603 into a tilting 'pick-up' test-bed. It was fitted with projected APT-P power bogies and a somewhat basic pantograph, together with APT-P cardan shaft transmission.

BR

RDB998546 *Convex.* A purpose-built Freightliner outer vehicle, designated the title *Convex*, was adapted by Research in 1980/81 for evaluation in the use of advanced structural engineering techniques. The design adopted was specifically intended to improve fatigue life of Freightliner type vehicles, *Convex* is illustrated from its outer, or conventional coupling end.

RDC460000. This rather strange looking vehicle, classified under TOPS as ZXR was purpose-built by Research as a structure gauging (optical) vehicle, able, via its internal software, to establish vehicle/structure clearances whilst travelling at speeds up to 45mph. After No. RDC460000 was assembled and thoroughly tested, the vehicle, in company with No RDB975081 and RDB975280 was transferred to the Civil Engineer's fleet.

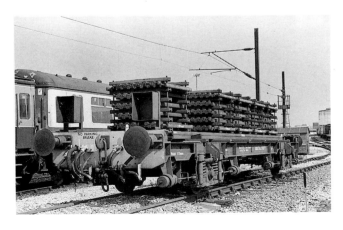

RDB511023 HSFV1. Built to the same basic design as a Conflat vehicle, this wagon was constructed to Research requirements as a test-bed for high speed freight vehicle suspensions and subsequently modified for curving tests. To add weight, special 'rail-packs' are carried. HSFV1 is illustrated in the Research yard.

RDB999900. This COV AB is another purpose-built research vehicle constructed in 1970 by BREL and fitted out to Research specification as the test vehicle for the TRIB train. The most noticeable external difference to a conventional COV AB is the provision of end gangways and a heavily modified suspension system. Internally the vehicle is fitted with hydraulic packs and special brake actuator units above each axle, as well as tanks and control equipment for fluid laying, used to induce/inhibit wheel slip/slide. When first introduced No. RDB999900 was painted in bauxite brown. This was later amended to Research blue/red, and currently carries the latest Research grey/red livery.

(Top) BR

IUO24497. Few internal user vehicles exist within the Research fleet – and those that do are used for stores. No. 024497, located to the rear of Hartley House, is a former CCT, No. 94507. The livery applied is Research blue/red.

IUO24296. This internal user vehicle, used as an oil store, was formerly 45 ton tank wagon No. A6090. The vehicle is now mounted on its own length of track, adjacent to the Track Laboratory and painted in the latest Research department livery.

POP/PILOT/POP. The skeletal POP train, constructed by Research for the study of tilting vehicles in preparation for the APT-E project, produced a most unusual looking train, which was later strengthened with a pre-production APT articulated vehicle *(PILOT)*. This illustration shows the POP train under construction. Note the vacuum train brake equipment.

BR

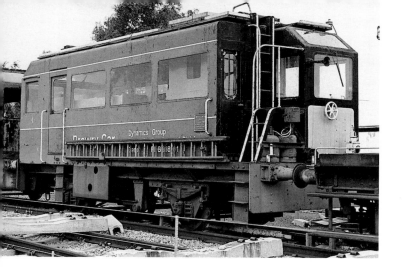

RDB998900 and RDB998901. Two Drewry Cars, built for the Manchester/Sheffield/Wath overhead system, passed into Research use during the late 1960s as overhead line maintenance/inspection vehicles. Today only one, No. RDB998901, remains active, carrying the name *Drewry Car*, and is usually stabled within the compound at Old Dalby. The second vehicle, No. RDB998900, is all but a wreck, dumped at the Old Dalby site and used for spares. The upper view shows the active vehicle while the lower plate illustrates No. RDB998900.

RDB965344 DRC730J. Research purchased a Mercedes-Benz 'Unimog' vehicle during the mid 1970s for APT-E development work, the vehicle being used on a number of occasions to haul the APT-E within the confines of Derby RTC. 'Unimog' allocated road vehicle number DRC730J and railway vehicle number RDB965344 is still within the Research fleet and used regularly. This illustration shows the 'Unimog' in its rail mode, hauling a 'Lowmac' with a camera-fitted road vehicle, in connection with the shooting of a TV commercial in the 1970s.

BR

JCH369K. In addition to the railborne Research fleet a total of three road vehicles are owned by the Division. One, No. JCH369K is equipped as an instrumentation vehicle used for gathering data at trackside sites. JCH369K is illustrated in the Research yard with the Division's 'Unimog' in the foreground.

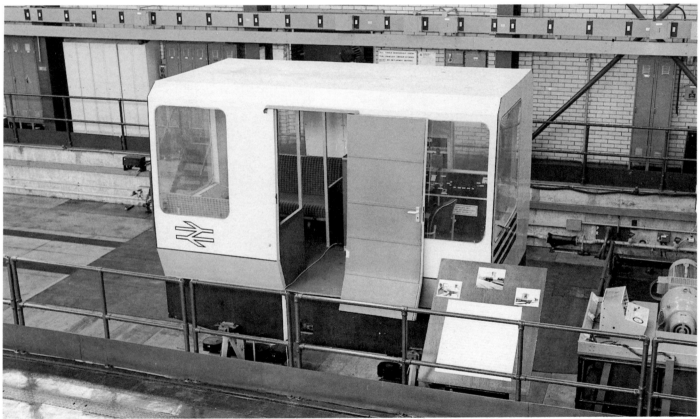

MAG-LEV. Research was, for many years, actively involved in the magnetically levitated vehicle project. To put Research Division theories into practice a *MAG-LEV* vehicle and short test 'track' was built at Derby. Following much work at Derby into power and retardation systems, the Division served as consultant engineers to the British consortium People Mover Group involved in the Birmingham Airport MAG-LEV project. The upper picture shows the *MAG-LEV* car inside the Engineering Test Hall soon after construction, painted in orange and tan, whilst the lower view shows the vehicle on the test track.

APT-E: PC1, TC1, TC2, PC2. Without doubt, the most impressive of the Research owned trains was the gas-turbine powered Advanced Passenger Train – Experimental, of which much detail can be found earlier in this title.

BR

RDW7258 DR73116. Track research forms a major part of the present Research function, essential with the quest for improved passenger comfort and higher speed. Research rebuilt Tamper No. RDW7258 as a pneumatic ballast injection machine (stoneblower), whereby stone was pneumatically injected under sleepers and trackwork, considerably improving previous tamping practices.

BR

DB96, DX74407. This rather aged Rolls-Royce engined Plasser & Theurer 06-32 duomatic tamper is the property of Research and used in conjunction with track development operations.